SURVIVAL

AND

ADAPTATION

The Changing Role of the Public School Superintendent

_____

Michael W. Jolin, Ph.D.
Superintendent of Schools
Johnston, Rhode Island

Rhode Island Association of School
Committees
Providence, Rhode Island

Survival and Adaptation
The Changing Role of the
Public School Superintendent

A Publication of the
Rhode Island Association of School Committees

Contents

Foreword

Michael Jolin's recollections as a school superintendent are more than just a reminiscence of his tenure as a school administrator. They are a practical guide for school superintendents and school boards. The pressures facing our nation's schools have increased dramatically in recent years. Schools are being asked to do more with fewer and fewer resources. Dr. Jolin's book takes a realistic approach to school leadership and governance.

Rather than preach to school boards that they should not micro-manage, Jolin realizes that school boards are by and large elected officials who are subject to enormous pressures. External organizations are constantly petitioning school boards to act on their self-serving interests. Whether they may be angry parents, taxpayers, elected officials, or religious groups, all come to the table with an agenda that they expect to be met.

Having read countless books, dealing with school governance and/or school board/superintendent relations, I am acutely aware of the need for a book that addresses the distasteful, but all too real, issues of collective bargaining negotiations, union grievances, interscholastic athletic disputes, patronage requests, criminal actions by staff, etc. While Mike Jolin's book recognizes that the priority of school governance is about improving student performance, it also addresses everyday concerns that any superintendent or school committee can expect to deal with.

Too many education advocates talk from an ivory tower mentality and proscribe plans having little to do with practical day-to-day issues. They expect boards and superintendents to be vestal virgins ignoring questions of local taxation or concerns of parent groups. These education gurus who often admonish school boards to be policy makers probably have never received a phone call at dinner time, from an irate parent, demanding the clean-up of a school playground.

Merely stating how ideal school governance should work does not prepare a superintendent or school committee to deal with the actual operations of a school district. Mike Jolin's experiences serve as a road map for would-be administrators. He depicts how outstanding leadership from a superintendent can inspire a school board to assume more of a policy making role. Good board/superintendent relations arise when the school board has confidence in the leadership skills of the superintendent. Mike Jolin's ability to recognize and overcome the roadblocks to successful school district governance can serve as a model to both superintendents and school boards for achieving effective team leadership.

Timothy C. Duffy
Executive Director
Rhode Island Association of School Committees

Personal Notes

The words comprising the first part of my work, <u>Survival and Adaptation</u>, are most often used in reverse. In most uses of these words, people are characterized as first adapting to environmental conditions either consciously or unconsciously as a means of surviving crisis. My experience of public school administration, however, suggests the opposite is often true. School administrators and especially superintendents, tend to survive crises and then adjust, modify their positions on issues, and adapt so that they may continue productively in their work. In most school districts across the country, the process is a familiar one as too often the parties involved -- teachers, parents, superintendents, commissioners, school boards, unions, and citizens talk at one another and allow problems to continue until they reach crisis proportions.

Daniel Yankelovich, Chairman of Public Agenda (1999) suggests that such miscommunication combined with high levels of anxiety surrounding school improvement issues lead to bursts and spasms of short-term problem solving and reform efforts that often stall before real institutional change occurs. School boards and especially public school superintendents are often the targets of related public frustration. The role strains experienced by incumbents in these positions can be overwhelming. The limited average tenure of superintendents throughout the country attests to these strains.

At times, it is easy to fall into the negativity trap. As I will argue throughout this book, however, progress will continue to be made as we work to improve our schools. Embracing the values of trust, mutual respect and patience by school boards, teachers, administrators, parents and students is central to this progress. Some will say that mine is a simplistic view. I believe, however, that those on the front lines of education reform will argue there is no other way.

Acknowledgments

In addition to my personal accounts and recommendations, the discussion to follow is grounded in current research literature, the work of the National School Board Association and the American Federation of Teachers whose perspectives have helped shape my thinking. The opinions of education program and policy experts like Barry Jentz, Joseph McDonald, Robert Evans, and Theodore Sizer also inform the discussion.

Further, I also posthumously thank my best teachers, Professors Martin U. Martel and Basil Zimmer who helped me immeasurably during my graduate work at Brown University and reinforced my belief in the importance of the values of trust, mutual respect and patience in constructively addressing public policy issues.

Acknowledgment is also affectionately due to my colleagues David Raiche and Michael Petrarca, Tom Bruce, Gail Keene, Martha Taylor, Brenda Faella, Steve Pereira, Richard Hilton, Michelle Ricci, Don Vanasse, Josephine Kelleher and Nancy Sullivan, and Michael Troffi. Also, special thanks to Michelle Colozzo and Livia Giroux, without whose hard work and tireless energy, this project could not have been completed.

Finally, lasting gratitude to my son, Andrew (a high school senior), and my wife, Diane Jolin (a fifth grade special education teacher) who not only supported me most patiently during this project, but also provided inspiration and much needed constructive criticism. And, thanks, Mom.

Introduction

My phone rang at 4:30 A.M. as it often does on cold New England mornings during the months of January and February. The call disturbed my wife's rest, but she was her usual supportive self. The call was from Eugene, our school district's facilities director. His message was a familiar one, "It doesn't look good. The Highway Department has finished plowing and sanding, and the roads are slippery." I told Gene that I would call my superintendent colleagues in our two neighboring school districts and get back to him within the half-hour.

Before I could make these calls, my phone rang again. A fellow superintendent, Bob, from neighboring Warwick was calling. "Mike, what do you think?"

"What are you going to do, a one-hour delay or no school? Mike, I think this is a tough one. There are about four or five inches of snow, and now it has changed to freezing rain. The weather forecast says rain and temperatures in the 40's by noon. It's real bad now, but it should get better. Call me back in ten minutes."

This morning I was thinking as I often do on snowy days. Why do I do this job? It's just too much responsibility. No matter which decision one makes, someone will be angry. One of a superintendent's worst fears is to make a quick "no school call" and then have sunshine at 10:00 A.M. Children stay at home, play in their neighborhoods, and parents and teachers question the superintendent's judgment.

On this day, I agreed with my colleagues and delayed school by one hour and canceled morning kindergarten and pre-school. I, as well as my colleagues, then checked out the "television scoreboard" to determine where our decisions fell in the matrix of Rhode Island's 37 school districts to determine who had opted for "no school" or a delay. Today the score was almost tied. About half the districts in the state, mostly in the northern area, had canceled school while those in the central and southern areas, where I was located, had opted for the delay. We had made the right call! This time.

The "no school" decision, more than most others, defines the role and pressures faced by a superintendent of schools. Safety, community perceptions, and the opinions of school board members, teachers, administrators, and parents all come into play. These same forces are at work as the superintendent considers issues related to teaching and learning. The ability of a superintendent to communicate and negotiate effectively with school board members and related constituencies while clearly articulating a realistic vision of school improvement and reform is the key to his or her success.

The role of a superintendent, from my perception, is best described as a tight rope walker who constantly shifts balance to satisfy diverse constituencies. School committees, administrators, parents, teachers, and others expect information and action. Each group has different priorities.

The superintendent must weigh each point of view, determine what is in the best interest of students, advocate for that position, and maintain balance. Each group involved in public education has its own power, privileges, demands, and authority. To align oneself with one stakeholder, defer to a particular position, or overemphasize the position of a single group, other than students who must come first, is almost a sure cause for the failure of a superintendent, especially one new to the job. As a new superintendent assumes office, each constituency will attempt to influence policy. A superintendent must resist the temptation to fall prey to power plays and be an objective listener and problem solver. He or she must build strong, clear, and honest communication with all groups.

Often this approach to school administration is difficult because the superintendent will at some point have to take a stand and favor one group over another on a particular issue. The superintendent, when taking a stand, must convey the impression, image, and resolve that he/she has made the decision based on the merits of the issue not because of prior or existing alliances with any one of the constituencies. The superintendent, like the judge in a courtroom, must weigh facts, evidence, and precedents and "make the call." Sometimes the superintendent, especially a new one, feels like Goethe's Faust (1824).

NIGHT
In a high-vaulted, narrow Gothic chamber
FAUST, *restless in his chair by his desk.*

Faust: I've studied now Philosophy
And Jurisprudence, Medicine,
And even, alas! Theology
All through and through with ardour keen!
Here now I stand, poor fool, and see
I'm just as wise as formerly.
Am called a Master, even Doctor too,
And now I've nearly ten years through
Pulled my students by their noses to and fro
And up and down, across, about,
And see there's nothing we can know!
That all but burns my heart right out.
True, I am more clever than all the vain creatures,
The Doctors and Masters, Writers and Preachers;
No doubts plague me, nor scruples as well.
I'm not afraid of devil or hell.
To offset that, all joy is rent from me.
I do not imagine I know aught that's right;
I do not imagine I could teach what might
Convert and improve humanity.
Nor have I gold or things of worth,
Or honours, splendours of the earth.
No dog could live thus any more!

Outsiders often think that the superintendency entails great power. In my brief tenure, I have learned that one's ability to defer to others, compromise, listen, and react to all sides and, at times, seek advice before making decisions is crucial to success. It is tempting for a new superintendent to take sides, commit early in the fray, align with one constituent group, become a teacher advocate, a hammer for school committees who are anti-union, or be an advocate for principals and other administrators who often become the victims of a rush to education reform.

Here I must note that, principals, like superintendents, are in shorter and shorter supply. Related debates bring into question one's personal beliefs and integrity in forums that are often heated, public, and energy charged. I certainly have no easy answers.

In *Survival and Adaptation*, I share some of the experiences I found to be most meaningful in my work as an assistant superintendent and superintendent of schools in two Rhode Island public school districts during the period 1994-1999.

My recounting begins as I served as assistant superintendent of schools in a Rhode Island low-income district I fictitiously refer to as Wellton and then shifts to Westwood (not the town's real name) where I began my first job as superintendent of schools. In addition to changing the names of these towns, names of individuals referred to throughout the text have been changed to protect confidentiality.

Unlike most public school administrators in the United States, I do not hold a degree in education or in education administration. My doctoral degree is in sociology, as are my master's and bachelor's degrees. Since 1974, I have worked as an Assistant Dean of Students at the college level and as an administrator in state level education posts.

Given my background, I would expect that critical readers might ask the question, "How is it possible that I have developed the knowledge base to address the day-to-day demands of teachers, who in many cases have more than 20 years of experience in their roles, and serve as an effective superintendent?" Contrary to such views, I believe that my diverse past is a positive and valuable asset enabling me to deal with the challenges a superintendent faces and helped me to work as a catalyst for systemic change.

Successful superintendents must constantly shift from deliberate decision-making models, tough negotiating stances, and long-term planning approaches, to quick, on the spot, problem solving. Successful superintendents must also engage in risk-taking behavior and then switch to nurturing and harmonizing styles of leadership and communication. Throughout my career, I have learned that these behaviors are central to effective leadership.

This perspective on leadership is reinforced by Harvard psychologist Robert J. Lifton. His work *The Protean Self -- Human Resilience in an Age of Fragmentation* (1993) contributes much to the discussion that follows.

Lifton emphasizes that people are becoming more fluid and many-sided in their thinking about themselves, their work, their friends, and society in general. Often they feel themselves buffeted about by unmanageable historical forces and social uncertainties. As a society, people change ideas, alliances, and partners frequently. At times, their world and lives seem inconstant and unpredictable. To a great extent, their feelings of dislocation are due to the rapidity of historical change, the proliferation of mass media and, sometimes, what seems to be the breakdown of community.

A good superintendent, or for that matter, any manager of a large company or organization, as Lifton emphasizes, must recognize that one cannot control all of the actions of the individuals he/she supervises and appreciate the value of change. Critics may say that one is waffling or sometimes overly indulgent, but keeping staff, union leaders and school committee members on task and tolerant of each other's perspectives requires almost constant adaptation and compromise.

I agree with the idea that administrators and managers must all abide by the 80/20 RULE. Twenty percent of a leader's work on a project usually accomplishes eighty percent of the outcome. (Benziger 1997). Most of the time, you don't have to do everything. You must, however, almost always be flexible, and I would add, shape-shifting, to appreciate other people's styles and methods to accomplish the goals you have set forth.

Superintendents and leaders of complex organizations must often abandon expectations of control and recognize there are different ways to solve problems. Patience, resilience, and tolerance for differing points of view are crucial. A spirit of conciliation, appreciation, and support for the work of others is necessary.

A number of other works have contributed to this effort. These include, but certainly are not limited to, Joseph P. McDonald's, *Redesigning School--Lessons for the 21st Century* (1996), Barry Jentz's *Entry--The Hiring, Start-Up, and Supervision of Administrators* (1982), Anthony Alvarado's "Professional Development Is the Job" (1998), and the writings of Theodore R. Sizer, including especially *Horace's Compromise--The Dilemma of the American High School* (1984) and *Horace's Hope--What Works for the American High School* (1996).

Reformers throughout the twentieth century, according to McDonald, have squabbled recurrently about the purpose of school, and these disputes have deeply influenced its design. Some reformers have focused on knowledge, wanting to ensure that schools turn out the best possible students. Others, most importantly, have focused on the children themselves. Still others have kept the economy uppermost in mind, wanting schools to produce the right kind of future workers. Finally, some have sought above all else to use school to improve or reconstruct society.

McDonald's focus on the changing landscape of past school reform efforts is generally on target. His observation that there are a number of misconceptions and faulty perceptions about public education that must be "unlearned" is important. Most superintendents, administrators, and school committees must unlearn that personal competition in school is the only training ground for productive work in a competitive economy. If there has been an important change in my thinking as an administrator, it concerns this issue.

Throughout my college and graduate work at Clark University and Brown University, I was immersed in a culture of competition for grades, advancement, and recognition. I, somehow, however, managed to stay on the edge, but also compete. Only recently have I been convinced, and my thinking reinforced by McDonald's work, that many in public education must rethink their notion of the relationship between competition and achievement. Perceptions on this issue significantly structure debate among superintendents, school committees, parents, and teachers, so firmly, and at times so implicitly, that they are not even aware.

McDonald emphasizes the point as follows, "It is the public's commonsense perception that personal competition is a necessary training ground for work in a competitive economy." This perception rests on the assumption that the school's essential function is meritocratic, that is, sorting out the winners from the also-rans. The problem, in terms of the needs of the new competitive, according to McDonald, world economy, is that this winnowing may well winnow out the diverse talents and viewpoints that would be successful in the new economy.

In addition to grounding my efforts in McDonald's work, I have also selected Jentz's *Entry* (1982), for its provocative and pragmatic focus. His work is especially valuable because of its stated intent, "not to try to capture the full tone of the administrative experience--the loose ends, unexpected crises, the affectionate, 'general messiness of any administrator's day-to-day life'--but to extract from this chaotic background, the elements of the experience of planning and process that are most meaningful." Following Jentz's lead, the remainder of this book is planned as follows:

Chapter 1 focuses on a retrospective self-analysis of my first assistant superintendency and supervision of three controversial projects in Wellton during the period 1994-1996: (1) implementation of the district's first comprehensive "management study," (2) coordination of the district's long-term strategic planning process, and (3) resolution of a long-standing salary dispute between the district's elementary and secondary school principals and school committee. My review of these projects is grounded in a discussion of related research literature. The intent is to capture a pattern of shape-shifting on my part and describe the evolution of my administrative practices in a way that will be valuable to others considering a career in central office administration.

Following Jentz's lead, in Chapter 2, I detail incidents, perceptions, and experiences of my quick transition from the role of assistant superintendent to my "entry" into the role of superintendent. This chapter, in addition to focusing on day-to-day issues, also considers the social and political climate concerning the search, hiring, and orientation processes for new superintendents.

Too often educational researchers and policy makers are far removed from day-to-day practice. Much of this is explained by the fact that few active education professionals find the time to reflect, research, and write. On the other hand, few researchers and policy makers have the opportunity to actively participate in day-to-day school administration for extended periods of time.

Despite these challenges, one person who has found a way to transcend related dilemmas is Theodore Sizer.

As Sizer notes in *Horace's Hope*, "The angle from which one views schools matters. The understanding of schooling is found in the relationships between students, teachers, and ideas. Kids differ, and serious ideas affect each one in often interestingly different ways. Parents as well as teachers know this." Sizer's words are as ironically simple as the message he conveys is complex and multifaceted. One of the primary lessons I have learned during my student and work years is that quality education most often involves personal experiences and relationships. How we promote and, if possible, create such connectedness is crucial to the process of school improvement and reform.

In Chapter 3 entitled, "A New Superintendent's Orientation," I expand upon entry issues and detail some of my experiences as a new superintendent, but from a different and more informed perspective. The projects selected for review include strategic planning, teacher evaluation, and the implementation of alternative school programming.

In Chapter 4, following a similar theme, I describe my attempts to promote and improve professional development programs for teachers, informed by new and different experiences working with staff, union leaders, and school committee members. Alvarado (1998) captures this spirit well when he indicates that the "new brand of professional development and collaboration" requested by teachers rests on the need for new conceptions of how time and money are utilized. Professional development needs to become the most important priority as opposed to the usual small and sometimes little recognized part of a school district's budget.

In Chapter 5, I focus on the issue of managing the superintendent's time. Drawing upon related research, I attempt to provide useful advice to prospective administrators who will probably struggle to develop a worthwhile and productive balance between work, leisure, and family time.

In Chapter 6, I switch gears and focus on controversial issues regarding interscholastic sports, extracurricular activities, and academic support programs. Although these issues may not initially appear as central to the superintendent's role, practitioners quickly realize that they tend to dominate a large portion of one's time. In Chapter 7, I return to an academic focus and discuss issues related to student achievement. Here, I especially draw upon specific examples of how I was forced in my early term as a superintendent to address issues related to student versus faculty and administrative responsibility for student growth and progress. In Chapter 8, I discuss the supervision and professional development of principals. As most every superintendent would agree, this area is a prime determinant of one's success as a district leader. Principals in so many ways are the true leaders and linchpins of reform as we work to improve student performance.

In Chapter 9, I turn to issues involving the role of the superintendent in the investigation of sexual harassment and sexual assault complaints against professional staff. Though very controversial and sensitive subjects, I must unfortunately say that during my first five years as an assistant superintendent and superintendent, I had an inordinate amount of experience in these administrative areas.

And finally, in Chapter 10, I summarize what, generally, I have learned during my first years as a superintendent and attempt to chart a future course of productivity in my role as an administrator.

As the reader progresses through these chapters, it will become apparent that my selection of issues is arbitrary. My choices are based on the most pressing problems that I encountered as a new central office administrator in Rhode Island. The issues of focus in other places or other times might be different. My focus is obviously local, but I believe that the dynamics of the school superintendent/school committee/teacher union relationships discussed will suggest commonalties to other public school districts across the nation. I suggest that my observations are common to those of a well-informed "participant observer" who utilizes a research technique most common to sociologists.

As Howard Becker once suggested, "It is impossible for a 'participant observer' to objectively capture, describe and recreate the experience of those he observes and especially of oneself. At best, what can be expected is informed self-reflection that seeks to define one's observations through an openness to the thoughts and experiences that will likely be meaningful to others." Like Becker, I have tried, in the pages which follow, to be candid, self-reflective, and open to other interpretations of the issues and events I describe. My intent is to share my successes and failures so that others may learn from them.

McDonald, when reflecting on his role as an education researcher, distinguishes between two perspectives--"cool" and "warm." "Cool perspectives" are those of a detached party: what an outside observer might contribute to a school's policy deliberations, or what a colleague might say about the work of a student he/she has not taught. On the other hand, "warm perspectives" are those of an immediate party: what the child's own teacher or parent can say about the child, or what the school knows about itself. Like McDonald, I attempt to bring both of these perspectives to this discussion.

I try, simply stated, to convey the distance of one who has not followed the traditional path of teacher, administrator, or principal to superintendent, but the closeness of one who truly believes in the value of public schools and one who owes much of whatever success he has had in life to public education. While I completed my undergraduate and graduate work in what most would consider "elite" institutions of higher education, the basis of training and education that brought me to these institutions was public elementary and junior and senior high school education.

Robert J. Samuelson in *The Good Life and Its Discontents* also informs the following discussion. Samuelson addresses the question as to why the United States, the most powerful and most democratic nation in the world, is so often overcome by self-doubt and confusion. Questioning today's fashionable pessimism regarding public institutions, he argues that the United States has experienced great success since the Second World War, creating unprecedented prosperity and permitting more Americans than ever before to seek the American dream. He also asks, however, "Then why is it that so many of us sometimes feel so bad about our institutions?" He suggests that the answer lies in a paradox of our own making.

My reading of Samuelson and other commentators indicates that a large part of the present situation results from having become overanxious and to some extent disillusioned -- "not because we have done so little but because we often expect too much and too soon."

While it is likely that critical readers may find that my discussion does not focus enough on curriculum issues, my intent is especially to provide prospective administrators with a pragmatic sketch of political, social, and general human relations issues they will likely need to master if they are to have the necessary time to tackle the so called "real" problems of education reform. To ignore the political and social aspects of education administration, I will argue, is a sure formula for failure. The successful superintendent must be politically savvy, well-versed in the issues of education reform, and able to adapt to changing social, educational, and cultural environments. Sometimes the demands of the role are more than one could imagine.

Chapter 1

Entry - Assistant Superintendent

————————

My initiation to central office administration as an assistant superintendent, as one might expect, was not without political overtones. The school committee vote on my appointment in Wellton was three to two, and I soon experienced my first indoctrination to school committee politics.

Shortly after assuming office, I learned that more than one school committee member seriously questioned my lack of public school experience.

Concerns from other school committee members also surfaced regarding my salary demands. When I decided to accept this new position, I was willing to take a $5,000.00 reduction in salary. A request to the School Committee for "reasonable salary parity with my previous post" raised the ire of some members.

Part of the problem was that my salary was actually higher, by about $1,500.00, than the previous assistant superintendent. He had been a teacher and administrator in the district for some forty years. My position was that he and the district might have "lost touch with market realities" since my resulting salary, even with the increase, was still among the lowest in the state. Another hurdle to overcome was the attitude of one school committee member who mistakenly thought that all public school teachers and administrators were underworked and overpaid, a point of view easily understood considering his frame of reference as the owner/operator of a coffee shop who rose at 3:00 A.M. every day and worked long hours in his smoke-filled, confining business listening to the complaints of the city's economically disenfranchised. His criticisms and others like them would continue to plague my tenure in Wellton.

I noticed that this problem persists as one of the headlines of the morning paper made clear: "Mayor Complains about the Salary of New School Business Manager." The article stated that the mayor was upset that the Wellton School Committee had just approved the hiring of a new business manager at a salary of $66,000.00, which was $13,000.00 higher than his director of finance who had similar responsibilities. Such disparities continue to fuel public displeasure.

In *Common Purpose* (1996), Lisbeth B. Schorr provides a telling description of the crisis in confidence many urban communities are experiencing regarding the perceived failure of public schools and their use and "waste" of tax dollars. "The collapse of confidence," she says, "represents perhaps the greatest obstacle to the development and implementation of successful education and social programs." The perception of waste and failure, while simply not true, permeated the general public perception of schools in Wellton as at least one other committee member constantly "hammered away" at this theme. His criticisms continued as the district ranked low in education spending compared with other Rhode Island communities during my tenure there and continue to do so. According to the 1999 Rhode Island Public Expenditure Council data, Wellton ranks next to last when compared with Rhode Island's other 36 school districts' per pupil spending.

According to Schorr, the press probably plays an important role in fueling distrust, misinterpretation, and misinformation concerning the cost and efficiency of a number of public institutions and programs. Schorr interestingly calls attention to a national poll taken on election night 1994, which found that 46 percent of voters thought that either welfare or foreign aid was the biggest item in the federal budget, although the basic federal welfare program, AFDC, and foreign aid each accounted for less than one percent of the federal budget. The actual federal budget numbers and proportions for 1995, were as follows:

Social Security	$336 billion	22%
Defense	$272 billion	18%
Interest on Debt	$212 billion	15%
Medicare	$151 billion	10%
Medicaid	$ 88 billion	6%
Food Stamps	$ 27 billion	1.8%
Federal Welfare (AFDC)	$17 billion	just under 1%
Foreign Aid	$13 billion	just under 1%

To Schorr, the widespread belief that the antipoverty of the Great Society of the 1960's and the similarly held view that social investment simply does not work are false.

In terms of investment in public education, she cites the documented success of compensatory education programs and Head Start, which have begun to close some of the gaps between the educational haves and have-nots. She emphasized that the public perception of the near complete failure of public education persists. This was certainly true of my experience in Wellton. My introduction to educational administration in the community was not, however, entirely negative.

The role of a new public school administrator, as Jentz (1982) suggests, is the quintessential human situation. "When the hopes and fears of all the years are rekindled--when the dreams and visions of both the person entering, and the organization inviting, are aroused--when the anxieties of facing the unknown are at their highest pitch--when one re-experiences the ritual of initiation into the mysteries of a particular tribe--when the advent of someone new is believed to hold the potential for new actions and new results--when a human being is believed to be capable of making a difference." These thoughts and feelings influenced my outlook as I began my work in Wellton. Upon my appointment, I received numerous congratulatory notes and expressions of confidence. Almost everyone on the search committee indicated to me personally that he/she had made the right choice. Given that the search committee included representatives of the teachers' and classified unions, administrators, parents, and community representatives, I felt that I was off to a great start.

The school system that I entered in 1994 was in a state of chaos. It was rudderless and seeking leadership to remedy what most teachers perceived to be uninspired political control especially on the part of the city's mayor. Local tax appropriations for city schools had not increased by even one dollar during the four years prior to my arriving on the scene. SAT scores, dropout rates, and other achievement test scores tell only part of the story. In 1994, Wellton's average SAT scores were 437, verbal, and 383, mathematics, and the dropout rate was 27 percent. Dismal statistics.

Worse still, the city's fifteen school buildings included many built at the turn of the century, a middle school with an enrollment of almost 1,800 students, the largest in New England, and another elementary school with a rusty trailer that served as its library. The city's school facilities study reflected the community's general impoverishment. School busing distances (the distances beyond, which students must live to be entitled to busing), because of cost, were among the highest in Rhode Island at one mile for elementary school students, two miles for middle school students, and two and one-half miles for high school students. In addition, per pupil allocations for instructional materials also fell below state averages, and money spent on school management and administration was among the lowest in the state.

Despite these negatives, I was fortunate to work with and learn from a caring, experienced, and innovative educational leader, Superintendent Dr. Josephine (Jo) Kellington.

Dr. Kellington's agenda for education reform was basic, straightforward, and one that I shared. Build community partnerships, strengthen families, support teachers and students, and improve student achievement. The reforms she introduced are too numerous to enumerate here. They included introduction of a teacher mentoring program and strong effective advocacy for increased funding of public education.

Prior to beginning work as an assistant superintendent, I was employed as Special Assistant to Rhode Island's Commissioner of Higher Education. From 1990 to 1994, I served as Associate Director of a new and exciting educational support program--the Rhode Island Children's Crusade for Higher Education.

The Children's Crusade was the first statewide program in the United States to confer guaranteed college scholarship assistance to low-income youth. The program sought to provide much needed after-school academic support and intervention to an overwhelming number of students who would benefit and was designed under the leadership of the R.I. Commissioner of Higher Education. Beginning in 1991, all third-graders in Rhode Island were invited to join the Children's Crusade by signing a contract, together with their families, pledging to work hard in school, avoid alcohol and other drugs, and operate within the law. The Children's Crusade in turn pledged to guarantee scholarship support for college, technical school, or union apprenticeships to crusaders who were income eligible at the time of their graduation from high school. The early response to the program, modeled after the Eugene Lange I Have a Dream Program, which started in New York, was overwhelming. The Crusade was and continues to be a dream worth dreaming.

When I left the Crusade in 1994, there were over 9200 third, fourth, and fifth graders enrolled in the program. Schools, churches, community agencies, and over 6,000 volunteer mentors had stepped forward to help these children. Together as a Crusade staff, we had established 47 mentoring programs to serve 1,500 children.   Twenty-four Tutorial Resource Centers provided academic support to almost 500 at-risk students in Rhode Island's lowest income communities.

I returned to Wellton primed and ready to share my new experiences in program innovation, which I and many others thought to be cutting edge. Dr. Kellington's and my focus on building community support and enthusiasm for educational innovation, however, did not go over well with the local school committee. Although she worked to leverage community resources to implement her agenda, the School Committee publicly stated on a number of occasions its concern about other aspects of her administration. These concerns related to hiring practices, staff development, and a lack of a comprehensive strategic plan for the district.

The superintendent's focus on community involvement conflicted, at times, with the school committee's priorities since it required so much devotion of her time to community outreach activities other than those traditionally associated with the role. I am sure that the committee members cared for and supported Dr. Kellington's agenda, but, as I became aware during my first few months on the job, they believed she should place greater emphasis on the more traditional fiscal management elements of her role.

Implementation of the District's Management Study

The school committee decided that my role would focus on the operations aspect of managing the school district, allowing more time for the superintendent to carry out her community-based agenda. Interestingly, it chose not to confront basic philosophical differences directly with her, but sought alternative solutions.

Based upon an agreement between the superintendent and the school committee, I was provided with two basic assignments: (1) supervise the implementation of an external management study of the Wellton Education Department and (2) coordinate the development of a comprehensive strategic plan for the district. The superintendent, in addition, also suggested that I might work to settle a long-standing salary dispute with principals and other administrators in the school district.

In these three areas I learned a great deal about effective district-level public school administration and sometimes experienced failure. As Jentz details, many new administrators have a tendency to "jump" into new positions without clearly prioritizing how to commit their talents and energy. This was one of my major errors.

The school district had many problems; my first reaction was to address as many as quickly as possible. In addition to the priority areas identified, I was actively involved with alternative school programs, the facility needs committee, the technology committee, overseeing school busing, evaluating teachers and coaches, and organizing a number of search committees to hire new personnel. Combined with my concern to prove myself able and please as many people as possible, I tended to tackle every problem in sight.

The day-to-day pace was non-stop and included many evening meetings and weekend events. Parent, teacher, administration, and community leader meetings and phone calls dominated my days and evenings. As a longtime resident of the district, I was especially perceived as "accessible" by formal and informal groups as well as by the press and tried to respond to all requests as often as possible. A curious point for new and inexperienced administrators is that they are often contacted by the local press for up to date information; many stated that I handled this responsibility well, though my success, I believe, proved to be a double edged sword. I honestly believe my ability to handle the press might have caused some school committee members concern. Was I a bit too powerful?

I attended many evening P.T.A. and P.T.O. meetings, mediated disputes among parent leaders of area sports teams regarding the use of limited school athletic facilities, and tried to attend to the needs of parents who were "just plain frustrated" with the way their children were treated in the public schools.

The problems I addressed are all too familiar to experienced administrators. To one contemplating an administrative career in the public sector or to the more casual reader, the day-to-day pace and tone of the public school administrator's schedule is difficult to understand. A recently retired Rhode Island superintendent, whom I greatly admire, once expressed to me, "The highs are really high and the lows are really low. You really have a chance to help many people and you do, but there never seems to be enough time in the day to do everything that needs to be done. Somehow, something always seems to be left undone, and somehow, you seem to leave someone dissatisfied or unhappy with your work."

Every superintendent I have spoken with seems to have had similar experiences. The challenge of taking time to plan and trying to understand individual and community dynamics was one that I had wrestled with but also one that seemed elusive. While I did recognize the need to plan, I certainly underestimated the time and attention necessary to address the opposition from organizational and community groups and individuals.

A clear example of my lack of attention to these needs occurred when I initiated the mandated management study. I relearned the lesson when asked to serve on a Rhode Island Department of Education "ad hoc" committee on Alternative Admissions Policy for the state's colleges and universities. This group, comprised of Rhode Island's Commissioner of Education, Associate Commissioner of Elementary and Secondary Education, Rhode Island's Associate Commissioner of Higher Education, a member of the state's Board of Regents, and others, requested my opinion on, as might be expected, alternative admissions policies. It was obvious, however, that I had been asked to join the committee very late in its deliberations and that most important decisions seemed to already have been made.

One of the most important program changes considered by the committee was the following:

Content Competencies
Statement of Equivalency

Provided by the high school principal, the equivalency statement would state that material covered by the student in an alternative program was equivalent to or exceeded that presented in a related college preparatory course. In those cases when the high school principal needed confirmation on equivalency, college/university faculty will be requested to review the syllabi and validate the equivalency.

The change seemed to me potentially explosive in terms of the new responsibility, work, and authority that was required of principals. Present on the "ad hoc" committee were two principals of alternative and charter schools, but no representatives from the scores of traditional high schools in Rhode Island.

When I asked other committee members why no traditional principals had been consulted as proposed policy changes were developed, I felt I was viewed by some as an obstructionist. I had few allies sharing my concern regarding the lack of input from these principals with the exception of the member of the Board of Regents. I left the meeting feeling a little bitter and that I had been "set up" to serve as a "shill." Now the commissioners could say superintendents "had participated in the policy development process."

As I addressed the school committee's directive to initiate a comprehensive "external management study of business operations," I made similar errors. I realized the need to go out to bid for services, interview representatives from the various companies and consultants who applied, do reference checks, and review similar previously completed studies. My major failure, however, was not to involve those administrators "closest to the action," and especially the district's business manager who oversaw related functions.

In preparation for the management study, I identified a number of specific problems to be addressed:

1.   The payroll for the Wellton Education Department
        was handled by the municipal (non-school) side of
        local government but still required extensive
        negotiation with the education department to
        address teachers' union contractual provisions
        such as payment for compensatory time.

2.   There was no comprehensive automated system in
        place for tracking human resource functions.

3.   There was a great deal of confusion concerning
        the topic of personnel records.

4.   The district, with an enrollment of 6,500 students,
        did not have a human resources department or
        director.

5.   There was an absence of line responsibility for the
        personnel function of the organization often
        resulting   in   duplication   of   effort,
        miscommunication, and unanswered questions.
        This omission probably contributed to confusion
        at school committee meetings when the
        superintendent could not definitely answer
        committee members' questions as to staff
        deployment and related cost issues.

6.   Almost every job description in the organization
        was obsolete, and job descriptions were not
        revised as new hiring occurred.

        I now realize that by singling out these issues
without the business manager's input, I had contributed

to her perception that I was identifying her department as one with many deficiencies.

Since I was moving so quickly and, as I thought, so efficiently, I did not really invest the necessary time to appreciate her trepidations regarding this management study. My conception of the numerous problems under consideration minus her input in selecting an outside consultant was a clear failure to recognize the internal culture of the department. This lapse in communication is common and devastating in a public school environment.

The school district business manager, an incumbent in her job for many years, should have played a much larger role in organizing the search for a quality management consultant. With little personal involvement in the management study, she subsequently did little to make the process a success.

Strategic Planning in Wellton

My experience in strategic planning and policy development followed a somewhat similar path. Currently, strategic planning is widely accepted as central to the progress of public education reform and change. Planning in most states and school districts is, in part, based on the premise that teachers are so busy with the urgent day-to-day challenges that they are not able to reflect on and evaluate the effectiveness of their work. Strategic planning, while certainly not new to public education, has recently received much of its impetus from widespread acceptance of the belief that a more businesslike approach must be taken to education reform to guarantee improved accountability and efficiency.

Education reform, accountability, and efficiency guided my approach to strategic planning in the district. As with the management study, however, I did not take sufficient time to consult with key constituent groups.

Superintendent Kellington and I secured the services of a professional facilitator to conduct a public forum to initiate strategic planning. The facilitator invited representatives from citizens in the community who might offer their views as to which issues should be addressed in the planning process. Over 70 people attended the first public meeting and, at that time, the prognosis for the plan augured well. We received positive coverage by the local news media, and many local political leaders were in attendance and actively participating.

As time went on, participation dwindled and frustration increased. School administrators and principals favored a controlled, measured approach to strategic planning, while school committee and city council members and parents voiced frustration with our lack of progress and timeliness. One school committee member, in fact, especially contributed to this frustration by publicly complaining about the slow progress. He also pointed to the quick strategic planning process in the community agency where he was employed. On one occasion, he offered the comment that, "The way my agency completed its plan was that the executive director locked himself at home for a couple of days and completed the draft, and maybe that's what we should do."

I fell into the trap. Working feverishly for about two weeks, I drafted a comprehensive plan with specific goals and objectives. The plan also included over 80 specific action items and what I thought to be a well-developed timeline. The plan was to be phased in over a five-year period with first year goals specifically focused on team building and generating resource potential to implement goals and objectives. I presented the plan to the superintendent; her reaction was positive. The strategy was then to present the plan to the School Committee and the administrative team for input.

School committee reaction was also positive. As one member emphasized, "It is about time. We finally have a completed strategic plan." The reaction of administrators, however, was far less favorable. During administrative team meetings, principals emphasized that the plan focused too much on the operations side of issues, which is what the school committee wanted and not enough on curriculum related topics, which is what principals desired.

The principals were concerned that the district did not employ a curriculum director and did not provide financial support for reform such as curriculum planning teams. They requested assurances that funding for these needs be restored. In many respects, administrators wanted a strategic plan that would address immediate concerns.

As one principal stated, "Two things are especially missing in our strategic plan. The plan doesn't focus enough on individual student curriculum needs and the political impediments to progress in the district." I felt the same about my experience with the Rhode Island Department of Education's Ad Hoc Committee on Alternative College Admissions.

As the principal observed, "Every school is different. Children's needs are different. The strategic plan we have developed refers to the perceptions of too few administrators. The plan, had more administrators been involved, would have had a more differentiated focus on individual students."

She also stated that the school committee was too much of a driving force in the development of the plan. In addition, she believed that the planning process did not adequately address the political climate of the community and school committee, administrative, and teacher union relationships. She concluded, "The political climate of a community can kill a school system like a cancer, and this is happening in Wellton. For a strategic plan to be successful, it needs to address this issue."

Problems common to strategic planning, in general, also surfaced in Wellton. As Evans emphasizes in *The Human Side of School Change, Reform, Resistance, and the Real Life Problems of Education Reform* (1996), many teachers and administrators have tended to remain skeptical about the strategic planning process and have failed to participate in it fully due to deep-seated doubts about the reform.

In retrospect, it is apparent that Dr. Kellington and I erred by not retaining the services of a paid consultant to facilitate the strategic planning efforts. While budget constraints dictated that we not retain her services, the problems we encountered suggest that we should have made funding a consultant a greater priority.

Lack of solid backing from administrators, teachers, and the community suggested that the strategic plan would not provide the blueprint for change that we had anticipated. The planning process seemed to heighten the sense of frustration all felt concerning our ability to build community-wide consensus. Existing tensions among administrators increased, and a sense of failure predominated.

The district did not have a comprehensive strategic plan in place when I left. In subsequent conversations with Dr. Kellington and school committee members, it became clear that no one person was at fault. We agreed that we should have done a number of things differently. Alternative approaches should have included greater use of a consultant to help structure the planning process and stronger attempts to solicit more input from administrators, teachers, parents, and community members.

I also learned that attempting to obtain broad-based participation in a preconceived reform process does not work. Participants in strategic planning must themselves design the process. Participants in strategic planning and social change, as opposed to having their participation requested, usually feel the need to define the change process itself and on their own terms.

Recognizing this problem resulted in a change in my thinking. When I entered Wellton as an assistant superintendent, I had recognized the need for constituent participation in any change process. I had not, however, been trained or thought to involve potential participants in the actual design of the change process.

As Peter Senge suggests in *The Fifth Discipline - The Art and Practice of the Learning Organization* (1990), part of my problem was that "Most strategic planning simply fails to nurture genius." He suggests that this is not to say that visions cannot emanate from the top. Often they do, but sometimes they emanate from personal visions of individuals who are not in positions of authority. Most managers, when pressed, will admit that their strategic plans reveal more about today's problem than tomorrow's opportunities. Managers often use strategic planning as a "ruse" to force their own agendas for change. Sometimes this works but not often. My attempts at strategic planning in Wellton substantiated Senge's position.

Administrators' Salary Disputes

Issues of compensation continued to dominate the landscape as I gained my first experience as an assistant superintendent.

An excerpt from the community's local newspaper detailing one school committee member's response to Superintendent Kellington's request that I be provided a salary increase upon one year of service to the district captures the tone.

The aforementioned coffee shop owner, a committee member, said, and I quote, "Now earning more than his predecessor, Jolin's workload will now be reduced with the hiring of a newly proposed grant writer. Right from the beginning, I said I supported the salary Jolin received only because he was going to fold the grant-writing work into his job. Now that a new employee will be doing that work for $25,000.00, Jolin should receive a similar reduction in his pay. It's no reflection on his performance as assistant superintendent. He's done a first-rate job."

In response to the member's comment, I voiced disappointment at a public school committee meeting and argued that my workload had actually increased. I also made reference to the $50,000.00 in grant money that I had obtained and stated that the new grant writer would simply be supplementing my efforts. Finally, I also noted that it was "unfortunate that the level of discourse had deteriorated to such a level."

Acrimony regarding teachers' and administrative salaries permeated the climate during my tenure in Wellton. Principals and other administrators including the special education director, facilities manager, and business manager had not received salary increases for four years and ranked at the bottom when compared with their counterparts in similar positions in the state. Three well-qualified principals left in my first year. Lawsuits were pending and tensions were high.

Unfortunately, the school committee was in an untenable position having to support a sixteen-percent one-year salary increase necessary to bring administrators to parity with their counterparts in similar positions in other communities. From a political point of view, this figure was unthinkable. Expressions of frustration on the part of administrators included failure to attend strategic planning meetings, some school events, and public expression of displeasure through local radio and print media.

I again leaped into the fray with little planning as I had with the management study and strategic planning efforts in Wellton.

In essence, I believed and advocated for the administrators and lobbied hard with individual school committee members on a one-to-one basis. After months, I was able to help shift school committee opinion, and a reasonable compromise with the administration was facilitated. In retrospect, however, I now realize that I was likely a bit overzealous in my advocacy for the administrators contributing to school committee opinion that I was perhaps not as strong an advocate for their positions and opinions on related issues.

Despite conflicts surrounding the management study, strategic planning, and salary issues, my experiences in Wellton were certainly not all negative. I enjoyed close relationships with friends, teachers, and administrators and introduced a number of small but lasting changes in the district. In addition to helping to solve the administrative salary dispute, I played an important role in introducing a number of program improvements. Through the use of grant funds, I established the position of the district's first Technology Coordinator, rejuvenated the district's technology committee, and established trusting relationships with the district's classified and teachers' unions.

The relationship among a public school superintendent, teachers' unions, and principal compensation issues is indeed complex and involves the need for understanding. My approach to the issue is in large part grounded in W. Edwards Deming's work. Despite public discourse to the contrary, my experience has been that most administrators, teachers, and support staff want to do what is best for students. Too often misconceptions, false information, and sometimes fear influence decision-making. Undeniably the desire for quick and immediate change on the part of policy makers takes its toll.

School committees are under pressure to hold tax rates down, keep teachers and administrators in line, and advocate cost cutting. Many are elected on these campaign agendas. They have claimed to be the forces of change but then soon realize the complexities involved. Schools are at the forefront of social change. Teachers, administrators, and school committee members are the movers and shakers.

Deming, in simple terms, suggests that communication and trust are key elements among these groups while each one attempts to adopt productive approaches to change and program improvements. During my experience as assistant superintendent, I sometimes felt that the school committee did not understand this to be true and believed that a more adversarial approach to the teacher's union was best for students. I disagreed and continue to do so. Despite differences of opinion with school committee leadership, however, I always worked to keep lines of communication open and negotiate toward win/win solutions to problems.

My primary test in the area of trust, in Wellton, focused on the complaints of staff at the middle school regarding air quality issues. Faculty at the school were complaining of headaches, breathing difficulties, and general distress. Instead of pushing these problems aside, I met them head on with the superintendent's support and brought sundry outside resources to bear on the problem. I summoned state and local air quality regulators for air quality testing and toured the school with them and administrative staff on a daily basis until the problem was solved.

Unfortunately, we had to close the middle school for ten days and faced intense parent and media scrutiny as the problem was investigated. Ultimately, teachers' complaints were justified. In spite of all the outside resources brought to bear, it was one of our own maintenance staff people who discovered during the investigation that, oddly enough, formaldehyde was escaping from window insulation in the rooms in

question. Taking these complaints seriously as public
pressure increased helped me gain the trust of teachers
and union leadership. This approach lent credibility to
my role as assistant superintendent and helped me to
understand the value of trust and taking teacher
complaints seriously. To this day, I am not sure how
school committee members felt. Did they object or were
they supportive?   I am not sure; the lines of
communication were not clear enough for me to
determine.

Chapter 2

Transition Re-Entry

In February of 1996, Dr. Kellington announced her resignation. While I had hoped to assume her role, I was not destined to serve as her successor for a number of reasons. Some School Committee members viewed me as somewhat young at age 42, and assumed that I would be willing to wait and gain additional experience. I cannot strongly argue with their perception. They seemed to be of the opinion that it was their responsibility to conduct a national search for a candidate who had revitalized a district with problems similar to those of Wellton. Often this attitude ends up being counterproductive especially in distressed school districts. It is often referred to as "the Messiah complex," which assumes that some outside force will come to the rescue. This approach on the part of desperate school committees frequently results in the loss of valuable local talent.

Wellton's high poverty rate and dropout rate, and relatively low starting salary were part of the problem in attracting a quality candidate. The average tenure for superintendents in urban areas, according to the American Association of School Administrators, is about three years. The cyclical nature of the superintendency contributes to a serious candidate shortage. The best candidates can, if they so desire, choose a district they prefer. Under these circumstances, Wellton was not in the running to attract the best candidate.

In fairness to the Wellton School Committee, it seems that it had not experienced a positive relationship with Dr. Kellington and therefore wanted to establish an open search process -- one that would avoid any appearance of stagnation in the district's progress, complacency in the superintendent's office, or the perception of politics as usual. I am sure this scenario is played out in many school districts across the country.

While the search for a new superintendent was underway, I told the school committee chair, who was up for reelection, that I did not feel comfortable attending his or other school committee members' political fundraising events and would absent myself from such activities. This candid comment underscored my lack of experience.

One September evening, my wife, knowing that I had made these statements, prevailed upon me to make an exception and accompany her to a reception at a neighbor's home who was making a first-time run for a Wellton School Committee seat. In spite of my objection, I agreed to go. Imagine my chagrin when the chairperson was also present. He was justifiably upset because I was willing to attend the fundraiser and declined attendance at one that had been recently held on his behalf.

In most cases my wife's suggestions, during the course of our marriage, have usually resulted in positive outcomes. This episode was, however, an exception and emphasized the need for consistency and, if possible, the avoidance of school committee candidates' fundraising events.

As the search for a new superintendent progressed, it became clear to me that I remained a viable candidate, but doubts persisted among some school committee members as to whether I was the right person for the job. In addition to my social faux pas, the school committee's ambivalence, in part, related to the more general structure and processes under which it operated.

Throughout my tenure as assistant superintendent, it was apparent that the Wellton School Committee was a school board divided. The board was divided in its decision making, voting patterns, and overall view of the many issues it faced. Part of this division related to party politics. More important than politics, board members also voiced strong differences on policy questions. These policy issues included but were not limited to school finance, special education, and dropout prevention programs.

The National School Board Association, in its orientation guidebook for new school committee members, *Becoming a Better Board Member*, suggests that a school board divided is not the same as a board searching for alternative solutions to the problems it faces.   According to the association, a divided board occurs when:

- Votes almost always split along factional lines regardless of the issue.
- Members have deep philosophical differences about the way the schools should be run.
- Personality conflicts, political considerations, and personal needs guide its decisions.
- Members do not understand or practice teamwork.

School boards, in such cases, increasingly become the battleground for a host of social issues.   Badly divided boards, in turn, lead to reduced public confidence in education and higher turnover among board members.   Often a split on a board will occur accidentally, but the end result is usually poor decision making according to the Association.

My purpose in discussing the Wellton School Committee's modus operandi is not to judge the quality of its decisions, but to illustrate how divisiveness can affect a community in attitudes concerning public education.

The National Association, in its analysis of school committee divisiveness, emphasizes that one of the biggest problems of a divided board results from how it is perceived by the community and the press.   If the press senses a split among board members, it tends to dwell on what separates them and does not focus on the issues under consideration.

A clear case of strong philosophical disagreement arose among school committee members in Wellton and resulted in negative publicity involving the topic of alternative school programming.

Alternative Schools

My involvement with alternative education issues in the community began two years prior to my appointment as assistant superintendent and was the result of my work with the community's Parents' Advisory Council on Education (P.A.C.E.) This group was designated as a subcommittee of the Wellton School Committee and was comprised of one representative from each of the district's sixteen schools. The group, prior to addressing alternative school issues, had been active in advocacy to increase state funding to Wellton's public schools. It had attracted significant media attention and was viewed by many as vocal, demanding, and, at times, controversial. This characterization of P.A.C.E. is evidenced by incidents surrounding a lengthy editorial piece it had prepared for the local newspaper. The editorial criticized the town's state senator, who was also state majority leader at the time, for his lack of action on school funding issues. He, upon reading the article, contacted P.A.C.E. and arranged a meeting to discuss its position regarding school funding and, at the same time, to voice his displeasure with the editorial.

While continuing its lobbying efforts regarding state aid, P.A.C.E. also turned its attention to alternative program issues. Based on personal commitment and a clear recognition that something had to be done about the high dropout rate (over 30%), P.A.C.E. invested a great deal of effort into researching model alternative school programs, conducted site visits to such programs in Rhode Island and Massachusetts, and targeted potential funding sources that might be tapped to institute innovative programs.

P.A.C.E., as a result of its research, recognized that there was a group of students enrolled at Wellton High School who were simply not meeting traditional academic and behavioral standards. In addition, this group of about twenty students was habitually tardy or absent from school, disinterested in the curriculum, and generally alienated. P.A.C.E. solidified its position in subsequent meetings. It focused on the belief that early intervention and comprehensiveness were the keys to success if the needs of alienated students were to be addressed adequately. The P.A.C.E. committee, in February of 1995, made four recommendations to the Wellton School Committee.

Recommendation One: Begin an off-site alternative school designed to accommodate chronic truancy/ discipline problems from Wellton High School. In addition to restructuring the school day, this recommendation also assumed that students targeted for enrollment in an alternative setting would benefit from a companion school-to-work transition program focusing on real and meaningful employment experiences that would be included as part of their academic programs.

Recommendation Two: Expand and build upon dropout prevention programs at the Wellton Middle School. As part of its research, the P.A.C.E. group recognized that while important and potentially successful efforts were already underway at the middle school, more needed to be done.

Recommendation Three: Provide extended school day tutorial, school-to-work, and improved college counseling or guidance to the 175-200 ninth grade students identified as at-risk by their teachers. This recommendation, essentially, addressed the argument that Wellton's so-called "average" students did not receive the necessary support to achieve at higher levels.

Recommendation Four: Restore gifted and talented programs at elementary and middle school levels through increased in-service programs for teachers. This recommendation was based on the assumption that there were substantial groups of students in Wellton's elementary and middle schools who were not fully challenged by the curriculum. During the 1980's, Wellton schools attempted to serve these students through "pull out" enrichment programs. As recent research has shown, however, such "pull out" programs are not as productive as intended. This recommendation accordingly targeted increased training for teachers to enable them to incorporate more enrichment activities in the regular school day.

In addition to developing these recommendations, the P.A.C.E. group introduced a funding plan involving budget reallocation and grant monies that could at least provide for a partial start of desired programs in the 1996 school year.

The Wellton School Committee at its February 1995, meeting, however, tabled the recommendations of the P.A.C.E. group. One school committee member's comment, "We are already spending too much money on bad kids," seemed to typify the sentiment of the majority of the committee.

On the other hand, the comments of one member of the alternative school committee typified that group's feelings. As the committee member stated, "I am insulted with the school committee's decision. I am insulted because I volunteer my time and attend many meetings for which I must get a baby sitter and I get lied to my face when the Wellton School Committee says it supports alternative education?"

The Wellton School Committee's handling of the situation provided a focal point for my frustration with its divided nature and was indicative of the general lack of progress the district was making. I believed that the P.A.C.E. group had performed admirably. It had conducted thorough library research, visited successful programs in the region, and provided a realistic budget along with its proposal. Divided political sentiment on the school committee as to the efficacy of alternative school programs doomed the proposals.

Wellton School Committee disagreement over the alternative school question and apparent lack of commitment to dropout prevention I thought to be important were major reasons why I decided to apply for superintendent positions in other school districts.

Selecting a new superintendent is perhaps the most important decision a school board will ever make. Choosing to accept such a position in a given community is perhaps the most important career decision a superintendent will ever make. A bad decision by either party creates a formula for disaster.

The superintendent, the board, and the community must share a common vision. Serious philosophical disagreements can lead to resignations and terminations, or, in states where the law permits, a buyout of the remainder of the superintendent's contract. Serious philosophical differences between the school board and the superintendent, if not resolved, may cause the school system to suffer from tentative leadership, conflicts, and lame-duck management.

Determining what kind of a superintendent a committee or school board desires, according to the National School Boards Association, is based both on objective and subjective considerations. A board obviously will seek a superintendent who is well qualified to run the complex culture of a school system, one who works well with the staff, and one who will be accepted by the community. Good chemistry is important, and even subconscious impressions influence the match.

Spring progressed, and I was interviewed as a finalist in one of Rhode Island's largest school districts. While my candidacy remained active in four other Rhode Island districts, one of them, Westwood, seemed to be the system moving fastest to hire a superintendent.

I did the usual research to prepare for the Westwood interview, including a review of the district's enrollment, test scores, and student graduation rate data. Based on my experience as a resident of Rhode Island, I thought that I possessed a good understanding of the social and cultural aspects of this community.

Westwood, in many respects, was similar to Wellton and had a high dropout rate, about 30%, an enrollment of about 3,900 students, and was recognized throughout the state as an economically distressed community. In 1991, the Rhode Island communities of Westwood, Wellton, and Pawville, were parties to a lawsuit filed in Providence County Superior Court seeking to find the State of Rhode Island liable for the inadequate and inequitable funding of public education. The issues associated with that lawsuit are common to those faced by many low-income communities across America as they attempt to fund public education.

The movement to equalize spending among school districts, as Wenglinsky notes, has risen in response to the way in which most of them finance their schools, local property taxes. Poor school districts, made up predominantly of poor families, as a result net less tax revenues than school districts made up predominantly of affluent families. The Westwood and Wellton school districts certainly fit the profile of the poorer communities Wenglinsky discusses. The goal of the finance equalization movement has been to use state and federal funding to reduce the inequalities inherent in property tax funding by providing funds to districts that have not been able to generate as much revenue from property taxes as other districts.

This issue is not a new one, as Wenglinsky goes on to indicate. The outcry for a more equitable solution to this problem has been heard from the eleventh century. The pressure to equalize spending, in many ways, has existed almost as long as property taxes. In *Springfield Township v. Quick et al.* (Supreme Court, December Term, 1859:56-60), plaintiffs sued the state of Indiana for not sufficiently redressing inequalities in spending between rich and poor school districts. The suit was unsuccessfully appealed to the Supreme Court. The decision of the California Supreme Court in *Serrano v. Priest* (I) (5 Cal 3d 584, 96 Cal. Rptr. 601, 487 P.2nd 12141 [Calif. 1971]) also opened the floodgates for school finance equalization.

John Serrano, in that case, brought suit against the state of California on the grounds that there were wide disparities in educational expenditures between school districts and that these disparities were at odds with the fundamental interest of the state to provide an education to its citizens. The court found for the plaintiff, arguing that the quality of education a student received did seem to depend upon the " . . . resources of his [or her] school district and ultimately upon the pocketbook of his [or her] parents."

In 1991, the communities of Westwood, Wellton, and Pawville brought suit against the state of Rhode Island and made similar arguments regarding the inadequate and inequitable funding of public education. Their lawsuit resulted in a successful ruling for the plaintiffs only to be reversed at the State Supreme Court level. The Rhode Island Supreme Court in its decision recognized that serious funding disparities existed between more affluent and poorer communities in Rhode Island, but emphasized that it was the state legislature's responsibility to address them, not the court's. Funding issues continue to plague the communities of Pawville, Wellton, and Westwood.

Superintendent Contract Non-Renewal and Termination

My research as I contemplated a career change yielded another disturbing fact. The Westwood School Committee had recently voted not to renew and to terminate the contract of its current superintendent. While possible capricious termination is a major concern of almost every prospective superintendent, it must be emphasized that only about 2% of incumbent superintendents nationally are terminated from their positions in a given year. The factors leading to such terminations are most often volatile and usually reflect an almost total breakdown in superintendent/school committee communications. This was the case in Westwood where the school committee in May 1995, publicly recorded a closed session vote not to extend the three-year contract of its superintendent and in December 1995, voted to terminate him from his position.

One committee member offered the following detailed statement of charges of incompetency against the superintendent: "It is widely known that the superintendent of schools of any school district has statutory and contractual responsibilities. These are covered under Rhode Island General Law 16-2-11. Furthermore, the duties and obligations are also contained in the contract our superintendent has with the Westwood School Committee of the Town of Westwood. Mr. Chairman, for a variety of reasons, which I will outline, I move for a vote of no confidence in our superintendent. In my opinion, certainly since January, but in reviewing prior documents, it appears for the last two years, the superintendent has acted 1) in an insubordinate manner toward the school committee; 2) in an incompetent manner toward his duties and toward the school committee; and 3) failed to follow the reasonable regulations of the school committee, including his obligations under school committee policy, the Rhode Island General Laws, and the Charter of the Town of Westwood. Fourthly, I believe that there may be more misconduct on the part of the superintendent in that he has misrepresented situations to school committee members -- intentionally, in my opinion."

The failure of the superintendent, according to this member of the Westwood School Committee, included not developing site-based management plans, inappropriate handling of resources, engaging in unilateral actions without prior school committee approval, and revision of the school department's budget without prior approval.

In reviewing the incompetency charges lodged by the Westwood School Committee, most of the charges seemed to focus on a lack, or perceived lack, of communication by the superintendent. It is certainly not my place to judge who was at fault. In most cases where a lack of mutual respect and a reluctance to share information are so prevalent, there is usually an absence of ground rules as to what and how information is to be shared. Misunderstandings usually include incongruence among the parties as to how information should be used in making policy decisions and disagreement regarding their respective roles.

As I drove to Westwood for my final interview as the district's prospective superintendent, these issues and related questions were on my mind.

How could I even consider moving to a leadership position in a district where school committee/superintendent relations had recently been so negative? Even if we agreed on a plan for positive communication and mutual respect, would it quickly deteriorate into the negativity just described? As I entered the Westwood School Committee chambers, I not only felt the usual nervousness of anyone on a job interview, but also carried the unusual burden of prior knowledge of past school committee/superintendent problems.

The interview team comprised of school committee, teacher, administrative, and parent representatives began by posing basic and familiar questions regarding my professional and educational background and experience. Two other distinct paths of questioning emerged as the interview progressed. These questions focused on my views regarding alternative education programs and school site-based management. As I attempted to answer questions, I tried to anticipate audience reaction and had difficulty keeping the prior superintendent's termination out of my mind.

During the interview, I also took the opportunity to share some of the lessons I had learned from the P.A.C.E. representatives in Wellton regarding their identification of the need for more user-friendly schools. As one Wellton parent had conveyed to me, "Regardless of all the alternative programs we develop, students and their parents will not 'feel good' about coming to school until our schools are more accommodating to them."

I have grown to share this parent's observation and have grappled to find an explanation as to why so many parents find schools uncomfortable, unaccommodating, and simply uncooperative. Part of the problem is that schools are often not organized to provide services to the public. They are designed to facilitate the day-to-day process of teaching and learning, but not to share information about these processes with parents or the general public. Main offices are organized as work stations where clerks complete attendance forms, process purchase orders, receive telephone messages for teachers and administrators, rather than being organized to receive, greet, and serve people coming into school buildings. They also serve as the first-line of response for students facing disciplinary action. It is no wonder that parents entering schools feel that their presence or concerns are of low priority. Clerks are oftentimes overwhelmed with multitudinous duties and responsibilities, which may explain why someone entering a school is sometimes made to wait.

A complaint I often hear from many parents is, "Why is it possible to go into a department store, restaurant, or bank, and receive prompt, courteous attention, when we are treated so poorly when we enter our child's school?" My response, unfortunately, is that, in most cases, the sole purpose of the person who greets you in a non-school environment has greeting and serving you as his/her number one priority. This is not the case in most schools. Until schools and school districts devote the necessary resources and staff training to greeting the public appropriately and improving public relations, problems will likely continue in this area. Everyone on the committee seemed to appreciate my answer to this question.

My trepidation, however, increased when the interview committee moved to questions regarding school site-based management.

School site-based management approaches have developed a strong foothold. In Rhode Island, especially, site-based management has been embraced by the State Department of Education. The Rhode Island Legislature, as part of its reform agenda, through the State Department of Education, has mandated that all individual schools in the state must have a site-based plan in place. Most local school districts in Rhode Island have also adopted the site-based concept while a few still continue to seek alternative paths.

As I framed my answer to the Westwood interview committee on this topic, I did not know of the committee's stance on site-based management. I decided that I would be straightforward and candid in articulating my own views. I realized that my candor, however, might backfire.

I am and continue to be skeptical about the benefit of a pure site-based management model when implemented without a strong district focus on strategic planning, goal setting and alignment of school-based plans into a district-wide coordinated plan.

Site-based management, in its purest form, places decision-making and problem solving in the hands of teachers and staff--those closest to the students and to the mechanisms of school improvement. Philosophically, site-based management assumes that teachers are most likely to find change desirable and feasible when it responds to a perceived need. I share their perceptions.

Site-based management is currently being implemented in many schools throughout the state and nation; however, I have concerns that it is happening without the benefits of adequate district-wide strategic planning and, especially, sufficient time for professional development. It is necessary that districts focus on strategic planning and professional development if they are to meet the diverse students' needs.

Evans captures this spirit well when he states, "Of all the complaints most often heard from teachers about the difficulties of change processes in schools, none is more frequent than simply, 'not enough time.' " Whether it is site-based management, integrated curriculum, or new technology, there is never enough time to support innovations.

In addition, after more than a decade of experience with site-based management in school districts across the country, a growing number of studies suggest that this approach to reform has been largely ineffective in raising the bar for student achievement. For example, in an exhaustive review of the literature, Summers and Johnson (1996) concluded that, while relatively few project evaluations systematically assessed the efforts of site-based management on quantifiable measures of student performance, among those that did, all but two reported that site-based management has had no effect or negative effects on achievement. Furthermore, in the case of those studies that systematically isolated the influence of site-based management, more reported evidence of a positive effect on achievement.

In another review, based on more than 80 empirical studies published through 1995, Leithwood and Menzies (1998) reported similar findings. These researchers concluded "there is an awesome gap between the rhetorical and reality of site-based management's contribution to student growth." Additional reviews of decentralization reforms in England (Whitty & Power, 1997) and other industrialized nations (Organization for Economic Cooperation and Development, 1994) lend further support to the conclusion that site-based management has failed to produce significant gains in student achievement (National School Boards Association, 1999).

As part of my Westwood interview, I stated that, "Without a coordinated comprehensive district plan for professional development, I do not see the site-based planning movement having its intended impact."

There is also a great deal of evidence, in addition to these data on site-based management, that limited professional development time is continuing to impede reform efforts. Most recently, the Rhode Island Department of Education, working in cooperation with the National Center on Public Education and Social Policy (1998), reached similar findings.

The department's School Accountability for Learning and Teaching (S.A.L.T.) Survey, administered to more than 10,000 teachers in Rhode Island in 1997, has yielded a wide array of data available to parents, teachers, administrators, and the general public. In terms of site-based management, sections of this research on teacher reports of barriers to implementation of ongoing school reform efforts are most relevant.

As part of the S.A.L.T. survey, teachers were asked to select from and rate the importance of a wide range of potential barriers to the reform process. The barriers identified by teachers included: School and Teacher Readiness and/or Resources, Parent Concern Items, and Lack of External, Formal, Organizational Support. Considering each of these categories, Rhode Island teachers rated lack of professional development time and inadequate professional development offerings and/or opportunities as among the most important barriers to school improvement in the state.

Upon completion of my final interview in Westwood, I was told that the school committee would be moving quickly to hire its new superintendent and that I would be contacted within the next two weeks. I was offered the position in late May. The timing of the offer was especially difficult for me since the application period in Wellton had not yet ended and I had not severed my emotional ties to the Wellton Education Department and general community. I also knew that I had the strong support of many principals and other administrators, as well as the teachers' union in Wellton.

I knew that from a personal perspective I was at what Gail Sheehy calls a "crossroads time." In *Passages-- Predictable Crises of Adult Life*, she captures my feelings about my experiences with the Wellton School Committee when she quotes psychologist William James. "Probably a crab would be filled with a sense of personal outrage if it would hear us class it with an apology as a crustacean, and thus dispose of it." 'I am no such thing,' it would say, 'I am my myself, myself alone.'"

Too much had gone wrong in Wellton for me, my mentor "Jo" Kellington, and all who shared her community-based agenda. The majority of the teaching and administrative staff had welcomed me with the exception of the Wellton School Committee. The school committee seemed to want outside help, and I then realized that I should move on.

When deciding to assume a new superintendency, one should focus on a wide range of information and seek answers to a number of important questions. These questions include:

- Who are the movers in the community?
- What is the ethnic, religious, and economic mix?
- Who are the haves and have-nots in the community?
- What is the community's image of itself?
- How are the powers-that-be tied into the control of the school system?
- What major controversies has the school system faced over the last few years (Jentz, 1982)?

The general thrust of these questions emphasizes the importance of identifying the community's power base. A second theme is historical inquiry. Successful efforts to manage and change a system rely upon understanding its historical context.

I certainly did not have adequate answers to these questions as I deliberated as to whether or not to accept the Westwood position. My knowledge of the demographic characteristics of Westwood was limited, for the most part, to information referred to earlier as the community was party to a lawsuit regarding state funding.

I knew that, in this regard, Westwood was a low-income community and experienced similar problems to Wellton. I realized as I considered the power structure of the community that I needed to do more research.

In retrospect, I would advise prospective superintendents to spend more time researching Jentz's concerns than I did, i.e., do a spot review of recent newspaper articles regarding the key political issues and problems the target community has experienced; seek out the leadership of the community's teachers' union, if possible, to obtain its side of publicly debated issues; and, certainly, review minutes of previous school committee meetings.

This review should, ideally, be extensive so that one is able to glean a clear picture of the school committee's day-to-day focus, priorities, and "hot button" issues. I did none of the above as I contemplated my decision to assume a new superintendency. Two major factors influenced my decision to accept the Westwood's superintendency position. First, I thought that I needed another chance for the positive start that I had hoped for in Wellton and wanted to try again. I also believed that following a superintendent who had been terminated would be more advantageous than entering into a superintendency that had been previously occupied by a successful incumbent. The latter assumption was based on the likelihood that there would be better opportunities to fill a leadership void and that a school committee was not likely to terminate two consecutive superintendents. The school committee in such a scenario, not the second superintendent, would likely be viewed by the public as being at fault.

In May 1996, I informed the chairpersons of both the Wellton and Westwood School Committees of my intention to accept the position of Superintendent of Schools in Westwood and gave a sixty-day notice to the Wellton School Committee.

My wife and I decided to continue to live in Wellton since our son was an eighth-grade student in the Wellton school system and was doing very well and did not want to leave his current school. The commute to Westwood was not a great distance, 35 minutes each way, and provides me with a relaxing respite from the workday's activities. I must emphasize that there are many positives and negatives associated with not residing in the community where one serves as superintendent. The most obvious disadvantage involves the many evening and weekend meetings and activities a superintendent must attend. Residence outside the community certainly makes such attendance less convenient. In addition, a superintendent living outside the community is certainly not as visible and accessible to the general public.

On the positive side, I have also noticed that living outside the community helps one develop a broader outlook on issues and an opportunity to maintain distance and perspective. While residing in Wellton, I often felt pressured by neighbors, friends, and family when I made day-to-day decisions especially those associated with the hiring of new personnel. In my current situation, such tensions are somewhat reduced.

Without belaboring this issue, I must emphasize that it can be an important one. I advise prospective superintendents to have an open and clear discussion with their school committees regarding expectations for the superintendent's residency. When superintendents and school committees have strong differences on the topic, it is sure to undermine the superintendent's long-term effectiveness. Frank discussions about the latter issue are also likely to open channels for clearer dialogue on other differences of opinion between the superintendent and school committee members.

Chapter 3

A New Superintendent's Orientation

My sixty-day notice to Wellton provided a smooth transition to Westwood. While continuing to fulfill my responsibilities in Wellton, I also had the opportunity to attend a number of orientation meetings in Westwood with the existing leadership team. Easing into the Westwood superintendency was facilitated by support and encouragement of the interim administrators the district had retained since the termination of the prior superintendent. I owe a debt of gratitude to Dr. Robert Ross, Mr. Sam Almond, and Mr. Jim Diamond.

Dr. Ross and Mr. Diamond had at various times served as Acting Superintendent in Westwood after the previous superintendent's termination. Mr. Almond served as Acting Assistant Superintendent and Athletic Director.   A brief and partial summary of their backgrounds reveals the breadth of experience and talent they brought to Westwood. Dr. Ross had served as a Superintendent of Schools in Providence, Rhode Island's capital city and also had a successful tenure as Superintendent of Schools in Quincy, Massachusetts, another moderately large urban district. Mr. Almond had served for over ten years as Superintendent in Westerly, Rhode Island, and Mr. Diamond had been a highly regarded long-term high school principal in Rhode Island.

These interim administrators, though retired, brought a range of experience and energy to Westwood that few could match. Their calm, well-informed, and politically astute orientation provided me with a better starting base than I could have expected. Mr. Diamond, in addition to his professional experience, was a longtime resident of Westwood and supplied me with great insight into the cultural, socioeconomic, and political workings of the town. At the time of this writing, he serves as the Chairperson of the Rhode Island Board of Regents for Elementary and Secondary Education. Employing the great talents of these gentlemen was also a tribute to the foresight and commitment to excellence of the Westwood School Committee.

In speaking with other superintendents, I know that many communities have attempted to save costs during administrative transitions. The Westwood School Committee, in hiring these three talented individuals, evidenced its knowledge that sometimes short-term investment yields significant long-term gain.

The town of Westwood was similar in many respects to the Wellton community I had left. It, too, had been a victim of the economic shift that occurred in northeastern communities in the 1950's and 1960's. From the eighteenth century to World War II, Westwood with its many textile mills had been a haven for immigrants (from Canada, Italy, Poland, the Ukraine and other countries) seeking a new life in America.

A recent report from the Northeast and Islands Regional Laboratory at Brown University (August 1997) indicates that these immigration patterns continue to persist. The report suggests that these trends significantly influence the public school enrollment composition in the town.

According to 1997 Rhode Island Department of Education data, Westwood public school enrollment was 3,906 in the 1996-1997 school year. Of that total, 93% of the students were white and 7% were reported to be members of identified ethnic minorities. Concurrently, the district reports having 141 Limited English Proficient (LEP) students who represent 4.8% of the total enrollment. Combined with the 7% identified ethnic minorities and a large number of unserved "borderline" LEP students, the Brown University Lab estimates that Westwood has a population of minorities, LEP, and former LEP students totaling approximately 20%. In addition, almost 40% of Westwood's total enrollment is economically disadvantaged as determined by eligibility for free or reduced lunch.

This demographic data suggests the elements of a public school district in a state of change and possessing many of the characteristics of the more urban school systems throughout the United States. Westwood, like other suburban/urban districts, faces the challenges of poverty, changing family structures, economic instability, and limited resources to fund public education. These factors contribute to a high dropout rate and suggest the need for more flexible program alternatives for at-risk students. Antiquated facilities and the need for long-term planning tend to be the overriding concerns of distressed school districts.

Given these factors, two of the most important contributions of the interim team assisting in my orientation were hard work in completing specifications for a $6.8 million bond issue to renovate Westwood's high school and middle school and beginning of a comprehensive strategic plan for the district -- "A Master Plan for Continuous Improvement of the Westwood School District."

Friends and colleagues often ask what my motivation was moving from the Wellton School District to Westwood since the communities are similar. I cite a simple analogy: to assume a positive leadership role in Wellton was like being out on a P T boat during combat, dodging fire with few of the weapons needed for survival. My initial feeling in Westwood was that I was commanding a destroyer for the first time. All the needed weapons or resources were in place; my responsibility was to develop and implement an intelligent strategic plan of deployment and stay that course. A major force, in addition to the interim administrators, in ensuring the availability of these resources was the Westwood Education Department's Director of Administration, lifelong town resident, and sometimes savior of the department, Michael Peterson. My first introduction to Mike Peterson occurred when I mentioned to Dr. Kellington that I was applying to Westwood. She told me that one of the main advantages of serving as superintendent in the district was that Mike Peterson, one of the best in the state, would be my Director of Administration. She was on target, and many others thought so too, as Mike was voted Rhode Island's School Business Official of the Year in 1997.

The graphic summary developed by Dr. Ross, Mr. Almond, and Mr. Diamond reproduced on page 65 with the permission of the authors details the comprehensiveness of their view of the district's improvement process.

They recognized the need for a plan that would focus on the wide variety of concerns that influence student achievement, while maintaining a level of specificity that would be manageable. First and foremost, as depicted in the middle of the chart, they emphasized the need for training, data analysis, and team building.

Their focus also recognized the need to establish individual subject or planning teams and subcommittees, and the need for an emphasis on continuous improvement. Throughout this discussion, I have focused on the need for a team oriented approach and they certainly emphasize this fact in their presentation. Perhaps, most importantly, however, they also focused on the importance of school culture, and individual teachers' norms, and practices as crucial to the success of school reform efforts.

In a study I recently completed entitled, " Teachers' Participation Rates, and Perceptions of the Impact of Strategic Planning in Rhode Island" (Catalyst for Change ,Winter 2000) my research came to similar conclusions.

Previous research and many policy advocates have pointed to the need for increased teacher and community participation in school-based and district-wide strategic planning. As Evans (1996) suggests, however, public education's track record in the United States with regard to these issues has been mixed. Many teachers in essence remain skeptical about strategic planning and doubtful regarding its likely impact, although they tend to value the process when they participate. My research findings involving the opinions of 165 teachers were quite similar. Involving teachers and others at the school level is crucial to the success of strategic planning.

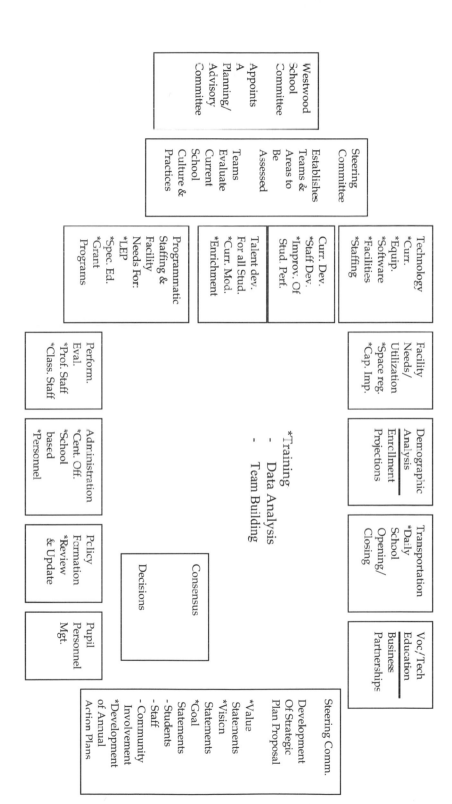

Bob Ross, Sam Almond and Jim Diamond, in addition to drawing upon their past experience, involved relevant constituencies such as previous administrators, teachers, parents, school committee, and community members in detailing their vision of ongoing improvement for the Westwood School Department.   Comparing my Wellton and Westwood experiences, one of my clearest recognitions was that I was "in the right place at the right time" when I came to Westwood. The chronicle of events to this point may seem somewhat detailed, but if someone is interested in working as a superintendent, this is just the tip of the iceberg.

For prospective and current administrators, school committee members, and other constituencies such as parents and teachers, I must reemphasize the need for an appropriate   match   between   the   choice   of   a superintendent and the community, as well as the skills and expectations of existing staff. As I began work as Westwood's superintendent, the school committee and I seemed to share similar views on important issues such as alternative school programs, site-based management, school committee/teacher union relationships and school funding issues.

Team Building

Given the controversy surrounding the former superintendent in Westwood, I thought that my most important role was to foster a team-oriented approach to all decisions in the district, placing student achievement as the number one priority. I emphasized the value of team focus in meetings with central office staff, School Committee, teachers, and classified unions. With parents and the general community, I tried to build upon existing strengths. People wanted to hear this message.

Community expectations are often high when a new superintendent is appointed. As I assumed my new role in Westwood, I knew that I should reach out to as many constituent groups in the community as possible.

Reaching out to administrative and teacher union leadership was natural since our views were compatible. Teacher union leadership had just witnessed the prior superintendent's termination and did not, unless dire events occurred, want to see a new superintendent experience a similar fate. This situation contributed to a positive relationship. Non-certified union leadership, for the same reasons, also wanted to develop a collaborative style of communication. Union problems were ironically not the ones that complicated or made difficult my transition to Westwood. Contrary to often-expressed stereotypes, I found both unions to be focused on progress for the district.

On the other hand, I found adaptation to the community's unwritten norms and mores a more difficult challenge. As my wife and son constantly reminded me, I was moving from a city to a town. One of my favorite classical sociologists, Robert Merton describes the related differences in terms of the German concepts of "gesellschaft" and "gemeinschaft," first expressed in the work of Toennies. "Gesellschaft" refers to more diversified, larger scale, impersonal, urban macro type social systems, while "gemeinschaft" refers to more territorially defined, closed systems and social relationships marked by common traditions and destinies such as those in a small town.

These ideal types became apparent as I became aware of the differences between the Wellton and

Westwood communities. Although outsiders might view them as being similar, they differed significantly in terms of urban/rural stereotypes.   While also differing significantly on policy issues, Wellton School Committee and city leadership as compared to their counterparts in Westwood were separated in large part by personal work schedules and time demands and their views of the community and the world.

The school committee chairman in Wellton worked full-time in the city and attended evening college classes in another community, while the council leadership worked outside the city. In Westwood, the school committee chair worked in town as the director of the senior center and also directed its social services, while the town council president, a retired local police captain and a best friend of the school committee chair, also worked part-time in town and met at least daily with the school committee chair. Such communication between Wellton School Committee and City Council leadership seldom occurred to my knowledge.

The school committee in Westwood, in addition, was essentially comprised of veteran members. The combined term of service of the five members totaled over 34 years, an unusually long duration in comparison to many committees and especially the Wellton School Committee. When I left Wellton, the total tenure of five members was less than fifteen years. Communication between school committee and town officials in Westwood was often immediate and usually clear in its intent. This fortunate state of affairs was in large part due to the consensus of opinion between members of the school committee and the town council. A positive outcome of this cooperation was that almost 99% of school committee votes during my first two years in town were 5-0. The trend in Wellton was most often 3-2.

The close relationship between the school committee chair and town council president in Westwood cannot be overstated. Their daily   s resulted not only in the successful completion of the school building project but also of several other projects. During a one-year period, Westwood built a new school maintenance facility, completely renovated high school and middle school parking facilities, resurfaced the outdoor varsity track, and constructed new soccer and football practice fields. In addition, every ceiling tile in the middle and high school was replaced, and the grounds at both schools were re-landscaped. While seemingly simple, as superintendents know, such projects often become mired in town politics and usually take time. Often the cycle of progress in local school districts is very slow as September quickly becomes June and another school year passes. The keys to our success in Westwood were communication, communication, communication, commitment.

While I agreed with the school committee on most major decisions, I learned to give in to their differing perspectives on certain issues or compromise to maintain the pace and order that we had established. The school committee also compromised on what was for me a major issue, my non-residency in town. School committee members often hinted that they would like to see my family and me move to Westwood. This pressure, however, was mostly subtle and not overbearing.

My greatest compromise was to give in to school committee preference to hire town residents to fill teaching and support positions whenever possible. The school committee's view, in essence, was to hire Westwood residents whenever the competition was close. I preferred to hire the top candidate regardless of residence but compromised when local candidates demonstrated positive qualifications. When larger differences were apparent among applicants, I nominated outside candidates and received full support from the school committee.

While discussing hiring practices with superintendents in other communities, it has become obvious that school committee perception and involvement can tax a superintendent's diplomatic skills. Conflicting views have certainly led more than one superintendent to seek employment elsewhere. Communication is essential, as is the need for both parties to understand each other's point of view. School committee members being political figures are usually deeply immersed in community life and are under great pressure to meet the expectations and demands of residents who advocate for candidates to fill job openings. The superintendent, on the other hand, must put student interests first, maintain an objective stance, and at the same time, attempt to understand community life and expectations. Such community understanding requires participation in after-school and community events and listening to the views of many citizens.

My advice to new superintendents faced with a similar situation is ambivalent. My approach was to follow personal feelings and style. I immersed myself in Westwood's community life, while still maintaining a discreet distance. I attended and participated in as many school and community functions as possible-- fundraisers, athletic events, community festivals. Upon the request of the school committee chair's spouse, I even modeled in a community fashion show to help raise money for the senior center.

I also made a strong commitment to maintain my commitment to personal health and "stuck with it." When interviewed by the Westwood School Committee, I was asked about my outside recreational interests. As the committee suggested, it was important for the superintendent to have "constructive diversions in such a stressful job." I responded by telling the committee that if chosen for the position, people would see me running or jogging around town on a daily basis. Until a serious knee problem developed, I lived up to my commitment. Now they wave to me on my bicycle.

In effect, I tried to maintain a "protean" stance, willing to shift my approaches to problems and, where necessary, uphold what I perceived to be the most important issues facing the district. These issues usually focused on hiring practices, student achievement, and the need for a team oriented approach to related concerns.

Prospective superintendents, however, should be aware that a superintendent's focus on team building may lead some constituent groups to assume that cooperation is simply another way of stating that business will be conducted as usual. Maintaining cooperative relations while confronting and embracing the need for change is one of the most important challenges faced by a new leader of any organization. Usually the new superintendent is expected to facilitate change, and the reaction of staff to change is too often fear. Recognizing how to deal with organizational fear is central to the success of a new superintendent.

Senge (1990) in the *Fifth Discipline*, argues that "there are two fundamental sources of energy that can

motivate organizations: fear and aspiration. The power
of fear underlies negative visions. Many organizations
truly pull together only when their survival is
threatened. They focus on avoiding what people don't
want--being taken over, going bankrupt, or losing jobs."
Negative visions, however, are limiting for three reasons.
First, energy that could build something new is diverted
to avoiding an unwanted situation. Second, negative
visions carry a subtle yet unmistakable message of
powerlessness. Third, negative visions are inevitably
short term.

Senge suggests that the power of aspirations
drives positive visions. Fear can produce extraordinary
changes in short periods. An inspiration endures as a
continuing source of learning and growth.

Hiring a New Principal

One of the most important decisions I faced
during my early tenure in Westwood related to this
problem involved the issue of whether or not to promote
the town's assistant high school principal, who had held
that position for seventeen years, to principal. The
alternative was to conduct a broad-based external search.
This problem, in many ways, was fraught with
controversy and cut to the fear/aspiration debate.

The assistant principal's candidacy, in addition to
his years of experience, was greatly enhanced by the
support of faculty and students at the high school.
Almost as soon as I became superintendent, I received a
petition signed by over 90% of the faculty at Westwood
High School recommending that the assistant principal
be promoted.

I am certain that the faculty looked to him as a source of stability during turbulent times and believed that he was worthy of being promoted. Dr. Ross and Mr. Diamond advised me otherwise, and I took their advice. In mid-July, the position of Principal of Westwood High School was advertised; a solid pool of candidates emerged.

Interviews were held in August, and an unexpected result occurred. The interview committee chose an external candidate as its number one choice. The student representative on the committee stated, "I had come into the process intending to support our assistant principal but now I have totally changed my mind--Mrs. Peroni is so energetic. She should be our new principal." I shared that point of view.

Seasoned superintendents would find it easy to describe Mrs. Peroni. She is a veteran high school English teacher who began work in a large urban school district in the late 1960's. She has taught and counseled generations of high school students, has learned as a parent of her own children as they experienced high school, achieved, and graduated from college, and has remained an active career learner, honed her skills as an assistant principal and was now ready to make her mark--a perfect principal candidate for Westwood High School.

Before notifying the school committee of my decision, I risked phoning the assistant principal to inform him of the day's proceedings so that he would be the first to know. I also asked for his cooperation and valued assistance in the pending transition. It was a difficult call to make since I had never called him at home and felt that I was not only the bearer of bad news, but also much of its cause. Complicating the situation was the fact that his father was a former chairperson of the Westwood School Committee and an acknowledged though aging leader of the community. The assistant principal stated that he truly thanked me for my candor and that it meant a lot to him to be informed before hearing the news from some other source. He also stated that he would do everything possible to assist and work collaboratively with the new principal.

For a new superintendent, this situation is difficult to address. I knew that I had hurt the feelings of the assistant, but also that I had to do what was in the best interests of the district. During the next two years until his retirement, Dr. Lionel (Doc) Archer was true to his word, and I cannot say enough about his professionalism as he worked collaboratively with Mrs. Peroni.

The lesson for me and for prospective superintendents was and continues to be cogent. I made an unpopular decision, which was eventually understood by critics to be in the best interests of students. This point needs to be underlined twice. The success of a new superintendent often hinges on when he/she chooses to take risks. Sometimes one is tempted to boldly let the pieces fall where they may if one believes he is right. Usually a more cautious approach that solicits the support of related constituencies is advisable.

Prior to my being hired as Westwood's superintendent, a second vacancy had occurred at the principal level, which required another risky value-laden decision. One of the town's most esteemed and highly regarded elementary principals had decided to move to a principal's position in another district. Most townspeople thought his decision to leave resulted from his frustration with the acrimony surrounding the termination of the previous superintendent and general negative feelings regarding public education in the town. Replacing this popular administrator presented me with important challenges.

I took another risk and contacted a Wellton administrator for the position. He agreed to apply.

Dennis Garcia (Mr. G.) is difficult to describe other than to say that he does not fit the profile of what most would expect of the ideal elementary principal. Mr. G., a former college football player and my friend for over twenty years, is big, sometimes too loud, and sometimes a bit gruff; however, he knows how to run an elementary school. His greatest asset is a hands-on and visible approach when working with staff, students, and parents. No problem has ever been too big or too small for Mr. G. Parents, staff, and the school committee in Westwood have grown to love him. Other less personal issues, which I faced as Westwood's superintendent, included data analysis, management information, strategic planning, and alternative education. Certainly not as entertaining or, at times, as glamorous as Mr. G., they nevertheless demanded my attention.

Data Analysis

As I began my tenure in Westwood, the district's problems with data management and analysis, common to many school districts, became apparent.

The high school's dropout rate had been reported as 46% for 1995 through 1996. This statistic seemed highly suspect given the demographic characteristics of the community. With some trepidation, I publicly stated my doubts about the dropout rate during interviews for local and statewide newspapers. During these interviews, I pointed to the need not only to correct the reported dropout figure, but also to improve the data collection efforts in the system as a whole. These public statements were risky but necessary. I tempered my remarks with comments that the issues at hand were systemic and not the result of the efforts of any one individual or group. For new superintendents, this strategy is essential. Problems, as opposed to failures, should be identified.

All it took was a few weeks to discover that the district's 1995-1996 dropout rate was actually 29.6%. This figure seemed more realistic for a low-income community such as Westwood with its high percentage of at-risk students compared to Rhode Island's statewide reported dropout rate of 17.6% and would serve as a more accurate baseline for future strategic planning and dropout prevention efforts.

By focusing on the dropout rate, I was able to alert the school committee, administrators, teachers, and staff to the need for improved, data-driven, decision-making processes throughout the district and gain their confidence in my analytic and public relations skills. This approach meshed well with the Rhode Island Department of Education's School Accountability for Learning and Teaching (SALT, 1997) and Strategic Planning.

Strategic Planning

As I initiated and implemented a strategic plan for the Westwood School Department, I took an approach different from that taken in Wellton. Time and effort

were expended to involve key administrators and
community members to help define the developmental
process of the strategic plan. Key players were now
defining the process as well as participating in it.

During the weeks prior to initiating the strategic
planning process, I met individually and in groups with
administrators, teachers, community leaders, and
members of the school committee to discuss the various
approaches to strategic planning and the direction to be
followed.

One of the more unusual and productive
suggestions came during these sessions from Mr. Jay
Raines, Vice-President of Centreville Bank, one of the
town's leading financial institutions. Mr. Raines
emphasized, while explaining how the bank approached
strategic planning, that such organizations have two
strategic plans.

One plan is internal, detailed, and confidential
and shared only on a need-to-know basis. The other plan
is less detailed, prepared for public consumption, and
serves as a public relations tool rather than a functional
planning document. He further indicated that it would
not be feasible or profitable for a financial institution to
publicize industrial lending or land acquisitions plans
prior to the consummation of related legal agreements
and contracts. Such public disclosures, in most cases,
would significantly impair the bank's ability to conduct
its business.

Raines recognized that public schools cannot keep
their strategic plans confidential, but his major point was
that schools should pay more attention to the public
relations aspect of the strategic planning process.
Furthermore, he offered two specific suggestions. First,
keep the strategic planning process structured,

organized, and focused.   Second, assure that the planning process results in a simple, concise document readily understandable and available to the public.

Those involved in developing the strategic plan in Westwood took Raines' suggestions seriously.   They attempted, following his lead, to structure strategic planning meetings clearly and to provide participants with succinct information about ongoing educational practices and school improvement activities. A detailed agenda for the important information sharing meetings is reproduced below and could serve as a guide for new superintendents as they formulate strategic planning processes in their districts.   This agenda focuses on broad-based, but structured, information sharing and participation.   Some people in Westwood may feel that progress has occurred too quickly and that their opinions have not been incorporated in the final draft of the strategic planning document. I trust, however, that they will agree that strategic planning is a process of continuous improvement.

AGENDA

MAY 7, 1998
Strategic Planning Goals
3:00 - 5:00 P.M.

1.   **A Unified Team Approach**
2.   **Safe & Appropriate Educational Facilities**
       for All Students

3:00   3:15   **Introduction**

3:15 - 4:00   **Panel Presentations**

Need for Unified Team Approach
Positive Contract Negotiations
(Teachers' Union President)

Mission Statement/Community
Vision
(Middle School Principal)

Cooperative Effort
(Classified Union President)

Professional Development
Academy
(Acting Academy Director)

Policy Manual
(Superintendent)

Facilities Planning

4:00 - 4:15 **Public Comment/Public**
                 Suggestions

4:15 - 5:00 **Action Steps**

Year 1 – 2:   Continue to work
Cooperatively to resolve
labor/management
differences--Endorse and
refine Strategic Plan.
Begin implementation of
Professional Development
Academy. Revise
Long-term Capital Budget
and Facilities Plan.

Year 2 – 3:   Continue Year 1-2 initiatives.
Present bond issue to voters
for a new elementary school.
Improve security in each of
the district's schools.
Continue to expand
Professional Development
Academy. Refine Strategic
Plan in terms of the Rhode
Island Department of
Education's Strategic Plan
and Article 31.

5:00 - 6:00 **Break**

Successful community meetings made it possible to finalize the Westwood School Department's strategic plan in November 1998. The ten goals of the strategic plan are listed below and will continue to influence educational reform and school improvement activities.

GOAL 1   "A Unified Team Approach"
GOAL 2   "Safe and Appropriate Educational
              Facilities"
GOAL 3:   "Data-Driven Decision Making"
GOAL 4:   "State-of-the Art Instructional
              Technology"
GOAL 5:   "Improved Accountability"
GOAL 6:   "Clear Academic Definitions"
GOAL 7:   "Curriculum Standards"
GOAL 8:   "New and Varied Program Options"
GOAL 9:   "Emphasis on Individual Student Needs"
GOAL 10:   "Increased Community and Parent
              Involvement"

The general thrust of the plan is to ground site-based management into a district-wide framework. These goals require frequent assessment, reconsideration, and, if necessary, revision. As the initial phases of strategic planning were approaching completion, however, it was gratifying that consensus as to the initial priorities had been reached. It also became clear that many of those involved were interested in developing new alternative program options for students, particularly, charter schools.

Alternative Education Programs: The Charter School Question

Michael Winerip writes in "Schools for Sale," (*New York Times Magazine*, June 14, 1998), "In the new education marketplace, public schools are expected to sell themselves, and the burden of figuring out what is real and what is hype falls not on legislators or district bureaucrats or boards of education, but on parents." The strategic planning committee now focused its attention on the issue of whether or not the community should move quickly to establish a charter school for students in need of alternative education programs.

A successful charter school was already operating in Rhode Island. Prior to coming to Westwood, I had been a member of a team made up of parents, teachers, and administrators in Wellton developing a proposal to establish the state's second charter school in that community. Since 1991, as Winerip (1998) notes, when Minnesota passed the first charter legislation, thirty-two states followed suit and there were 786 charter schools in America, with 400 to 500 more expected in the next year. Each charter school tends to vary in size, mission, philosophy, and curriculum; most are run on a nonprofit basis. In addition, about a dozen companies have entered the charter school market on a for-profit basis, including Edison, the best known, which had forty schools operating in 1998. Edison's claims to raise student expectations, performance, and test scores are indeed promising.

I tend to agree with Winerip, however, upon reviewing the current charter school debate: "Even in the glow of newness, problems have surfaced." In New Jersey, for example, a small charter, Gateway School, suddenly had three of its four staff members, including the principal, quit after a dispute. State officials responsible for overseeing charters were caught off guard, and a monitoring team had not yet visited the school. In another case, a charter school slated to open in New Jersey in the fall of 1998 did not begin as scheduled, leaving parents searching at the last minute for alternative placements for their children.

The complexity of the general school reform and charter school movement hits home, as Winerip notes, when one realizes that the "sales pitch that accompanies school choice dazzles, promising to deliver more, better, and sooner, when the reality is that education is an intricate process filled with subtle challenges."

Westwood was not ready to dismiss the possible creation of a charter school. For the time being, however, it adopted a more conservative approach and invested time and energy in developing an alternative school-within-a-school with a greater chance of success, a Westwood High School "New School."

The intent of the New School is to pilot a comprehensive full-day alternative program for Westwood High School students not making satisfactory progress in the traditional curriculum. At its core, the New School's most basic assumptions are that it must focus on individual student needs and interests and, importantly, that student competencies be measured not by seat time (Carnegie Units) but by authentic and performance-based assessments.

For those students not progressing in traditional environments, these assumptions are crucial since no alternative program will be successful if they are forced back into classrooms with traditional assessment practices.

In 1998, Westwood's New School began with a class of ten students who received instruction in the core areas of English, mathematics, science, and social studies on a varied time schedule. Students sometimes arrived at school an hour late. The New School was structured according to the following goals:

> To draft an individualized learning plan for each student.
> To plan and implement integrated learning opportunities.
> To focus on project-based activities.
> To encourage reflective learning.
> To provide a mentor for each student within or outside of the school.
> To provide a nurturing environment focusing on each individual student's success.

The New School is based on the belief that a single model or structure cannot always meet the educational needs of all students and that varied learning opportunities and locations must be developed. The New School focuses on developing pre-apprenticeship opportunities for students, expanded internship opportunities, and job shadowing activities. The New School, in addition, believes that learning can be made more relevant through community-based lifelong learning. In terms of its vision for each student, the New School projects a path of learning that will be challenging, evolving, and dynamic. Westwood's New School, like other innovative programs, will require close monitoring and objective evaluation to determine its success or failure. Our attention to individual student needs, student persistence, and achievement will be the key variables of focus.

To quote Robert Evans again, "Real change is always personal: organizational change is always incremental. In the best of schools, with the best resources and the most skillful leadership, the time frame for transforming culture, structure, belief, and practice is years." Success will require the highest strivings and the most down-to-earth expectations. These familiar admonitions were also relevant as we addressed the important topic of professional development of teachers in Westwood.

Chapter 4

The Beginning of Westwood's Professional Development Academy
or
Changing A Tire While The Car Is Moving

Teachers across the United States consider inadequate planning and professional development time as the most salient barriers to school improvement. Their complaints usually focus on a lack of common planning time and limited input into designing new professional development activities. These complaints seem valid when their work schedules are compared to those of teachers in countries such as Taiwan, China, Japan, and Germany. Research, for the most part, supports the idea that American teachers spend much more time actually teaching as opposed to focusing on planning, school reform, and staff development.

The position of school board members, in general, is in stark contrast to teachers' views on the time issue. They seem to be of the opinion that the process of school reform and improvement is too slow and suggest that teachers and administrators are reluctant to embrace change in instructional practice and behavior routines. Successful superintendents must find creative ways to bring the two sides closer together.

Negotiating the time issue, as the principal of Westwood High School once said to me, "is like trying to change a tire while your car is still moving. You know what you would have to do but you also know that things are moving too fast and that the task is almost impossible. When you are trying to change something that is still in the process of performing and doing business as usual, it's very difficult." She emphasizes, to support her argument, that in private business or industry when major change is introduced, the entire segment of the business or company involved changes its work and training schedule. The management of private companies usually expect that production will slow down or stop temporarily, but that later gains resulting from innovations will more than make up for the slowdown.

A major misconception that I encounter in my conversations with people who work outside of public education is the view that summer vacations provide transition time for schools to implement changes. Unfortunately, this is not true. Many teachers focus on personal professional development activities or pursue higher university or college degrees over the summer break. Few of these activities, unfortunately, are integrated into school-based or comprehensive district professional development agendas.   As I continued my work in Westwood, both the time issue and the need for better coordination of existing activities framed the debate over professional development.

As I first approached these issues, I had to address Westwood School Committee questions as to what would be a fair amount of additional resources to invest in professional development and, most importantly, why teachers should be provided increased released time or compensation for their own training.

The history of professional development activities for teachers in this country has often not been a happy one, as is well documented by the National School Board Association in "Raising the Bar--A School Board Primer on Student Achievement."   Professional development activities are   too often short-term and may be what central office believes is valuable but not what individual teachers want or need.   This situation is exacerbated in many districts where there is pressure to keep teachers in classrooms during the school day.   Staff development is usually forced to take place during evenings or weekends when teachers are often tired and sometimes resentful of the invasion into their personal time.

There is no easy solution to this dilemma; however, while discussing this concern with School Committee members and union representatives in Westwood, I attempted to foster a mutual appreciation between the parties as to their relative positions on the matter.

I offered the view to school committee members that teachers as a collective body comprise a relatively unique group as compared to other professions and that this fact is seldom articulated.   To appreciate this argument, it is useful to consider briefly the sociological analysis of occupational stratification in American society. Daniel Bell, in *The Coming of Post-Industrial Society* (1976), states that there are two major axes of professional stratification in western society: knowledge and property.

At the risk of oversimplifying Bell's work, one finds teachers as a group falling very high on one stratification axis--knowledge, and very low on the other--property. This is especially true when time or the management of personal time is considered a property right.

Teachers, in contrast to other professionals, have little control over their professional workday or schedule. Attorneys, physicians, and accountants, for example, schedule, reschedule, and at times, cancel or postpone appointments. These professionals often have the opportunity to schedule business lunches and decide when their workday begins and ends. Teachers, on the other hand, march to a bell schedule. Lunch is usually no more than 15-20 minutes at the same time every day with the same people, and personal hygiene is a luxury dictated by available time that sometimes many cannot afford. It is little wonder why teachers are sensitive about the professional development time issue when viewed from this perspective.

Evans (1996) further elaborates on difficulties associated with the teacher's professional role in terms of its occupational framework or context. He suggests that if the emphasis were focused not on the theoretical discourse about education reform between academics and policymakers but on the actual occupational context of schools, the environment that teachers work in would be seen as basically uncongenial and even hostile to innovation.

"To begin with, teaching, as an occupation, is especially prone to increasing people's vulnerability to stress, reducing their readiness for change, and pressing veteran practitioners toward the lower end of the growth and performance continuum rather than lifting them toward higher professional engagement and functioning."

Drawing on related research literature, Evans suggests that there are seven elements of the teacher's occupational role and work environment that make ongoing productive professional development difficult.

- *Social complexity.* Teachers participate in hundreds, and even thousands of interactions per day, from the most mundane (greeting students in the corridor) to the most complex (encouraging students to reflect on challenging problems.)

- *Multiplicity.* Teachers are almost always doing more than one thing at a time and must often switch rapidly between roles. They may reflect about their teaching before or after a class, but not during a class.

- *Personal involvement.* Teachers must connect personally with students to engage them in learning. This is difficult enough when pupil-teacher ratios are relatively low; it is even more so when, as in many high schools, teachers work with 150 or more students.

- *Motivational burden.* Teachers must capture and sustain students' interest and attention. In this sense, teaching is closer to acting or sales than to other professions such as surgery or law, where client motivation either doesn't matter or is easily mobilized.

- *Public nature.* Teachers are "on stage" performing in front of an audience for hours each day. Unlike many professionals, they make their mistakes in public and have virtually no private space to retreat to.

- *Unpredictability.* Teachers can never be sure that the same presentation will generate the same response from class to class or student to student. Though this makes for a certain variety, it also requires teachers to be instantly ready to modify their goals and methods.

- *Professional isolation.* Teachers' work is conducted away from peers. Though many enjoy being alone with their students, this seclusion deprives them of feedback and recognition--a key source of support, of confirmation of adequacy, and of information that can solve problems and improve performance (Jackson, 1968, pp. 9-19; Huberman, 1983, pp. 482-483; Sarason, 1971, p. 152-169).

As Evans concludes, every profession, of course, has its own pressures, but these characteristics can make teaching an unusually draining activity and related professional development especially challenging. "It's not just the inherent pressures of school life that negatively affect the climate for change in schools. Most districts are essentially structured to maintain the status quo, not to stimulate their own improvement." This, I would add, at a time when dramatic change and almost anything but the "status quo" is required.

Recently, I participated in a work group as part of the Rhode Island Department of Education's Strategic Planning Committee. The basic charge of the group was to further refine the "action steps" that would be included in the State Department of Education's strategic plan focusing especially on the topic of professional development.

As I participated in this process, I was chagrined to hear that the group was still dealing with the issue of "time" and had not come to consensus on how to address this problem. The planning group, comprised of professionals from the University of Rhode Island, the R.I. Department of Education leadership team members, local district principals and teachers, and others, continued to debate the professional development issue in a framework that seemed to hold teachers to the standard of other professional groups such as attorneys, physicians, and accountants. My position is adamant when I state that such an approach to school improvement and reform will not work.

Anthony Alvarado, Chancellor for Instruction in San Diego, California, who is attracting national attention, hits the mark in "Professional Development Is the Job," when he states, "Most school districts, if they looked in their budgets for their professional development money, would have a hard time finding it because it doesn't amount to much." As Alvarado further argues, "You can talk all you want about professional development and have high-toned conversations about it, but if the money isn't in the budget to do professional development, you don't care about it.   And that's something for school board members, for superintendents, for school-based communities, for everyone, to understand."

In another one of the best analyses of the time issue that I have encountered, Mary Anne Raywid in "Finding Time for Collaboration" (*Educational Leadership*, September 1993), sounds the alert that the topic has emerged as the key variable in every study of school change appearing in the last decade (Fullan and Miles, 1992.)

This research emphasizes that it is the public's general perception that the productive work time of teachers consists primarily of contact time spent with students.   The remainder of a teacher's time, according to this view, is either a bureaucratic necessity, such as faculty meetings or clerical work, or a job amenity or benefit, such as a preparation period.

To achieve real school reform, Raywid argues, "Administrators, policy makers and the public alike must accept a new conception of school time if we are to be successful in our school improvement activities."

As I worked to convince the Westwood School Committee of this argument's merit, I explained many options to extend the school day or year to provide for increased professional development.

Raywid (1993) identified no less than fifteen good examples in place around the country on how to extend the school day or year.   In Florida, for example, the Gardendale Elementary Magnet School has adopted a year-round calendar, with three-week intersessions between quarters. The school then uses the intersessions to schedule two- or three-day professional development meetings for teachers who receive compensatory time while participating.

On Long Island, New York, school districts commonly set aside three to five days per year for teachers to attend daylong staff development meetings. To encourage regular collaborative sessions for teachers, some districts then reschedule the term. Five staff development days, when divided up, allow thirteen two-hour sessions, or one evening every two weeks throughout the school year.

Sizer, more than a decade ago, suggested that the single innovation that would best help schools would be to maintain the present school hours of teachers, reduce the number of student hours by one a day, and use the gained time for teacher discussion, professional training, and joint planning.

I discussed these and other options on many occasions with representatives of the Westwood Teachers' Alliance as all worked to develop a comprehensive plan for professional development for teachers.

As I mentioned, I agree with Deming's approach: in addition to focusing on interpersonal dignity, he emphasizes the need for an enlightened mixture of teamwork, shared purpose, and the elimination of fear in the workplace. Whenever I communicated or negotiated with teachers' union representatives on the professional development issue, I tried to keep these ideas in mind.

During the negotiation process, I was the beneficiary of a number of forces coming together in a fortuitous way. Information had been passed from the Wellton union leadership to union officials in Westwood regarding my cooperative style. In addition, I benefited from the fact that the Westwood School Committee and

Teachers' Alliance were in the final phases of contract negotiations when I began work in the district. The rancor on the part of union leadership for having worked the prior year without a contract was subsiding; an attitude of "let's just get things done and get off to a good start with the new superintendent" was prevalent.

Capitalizing on this mutual good will and the recognition by both teachers and school committee of the merits and value of professional development set the stage for Westwood's Professional Development Academy--one of the few of its type in Rhode Island.

The Academy concept came to my attention thanks to the superintendent of Central Falls, Rhode Island's only state operated school district. This concept, in its simplest form, involves establishing a district's own professional development school staffed by district teachers and administrators who share knowledge and experience with their colleagues. Information sharing is also supported by outside faculty and/or consultants from area higher education institutions, businesses, and other organizations.

The key element of the Academy model requires that it be managed on a day-to-day basis by teachers. I faced two basic problems in attempting to convince school committee members of the benefits of such an approach: (1) the basic time/money issue, (2) issues concerning teacher seniority rights. With reference to the seniority issue, school committee members were concerned that if the Academy leadership were to be selected on the basis of seniority, the school system would, in effect, be left with a same old guard type of leadership.

Unless one has worked in or is familiar with a school district for a number of years, it is difficult to capture the historical flow of school committee/teacher union relations. The following comments offered by the President of the Westwood Teachers' Alliance at the May 1998, Strategic Planning meeting typify the new spirit of union/management relations which had developed in the district.

He began his comments by stating that his theme was "turning corners" or "turning points."

As he noted, representatives of the Westwood Teachers' Alliance in 1993 and 1994 might not have been part of this panel. He recounted how during 1993-94 and 1994-95, the collective bargaining relationship between the school committee and teachers' alliance was strained -- a lot of things went wrong. Tensions increased. Grievance after grievance was filed. Unfair labor practice charges -- one after another were filed -- and the union did not have the "ear" of the Westwood School Committee. "What did this lead to," he asked. "Possibly the most bitter contract negotiations in the history of this school district," he said.

"We wasted energy," he said, "and resources, and put a lot of money in a lot of people's pockets during that period of time."

"Finally," he said, "we found ourselves in a situation where we had new leadership in the school district. We found ourselves with a new superintendent, an assistant superintendent, and a school committee that was willing to bring the dispute to an end so that we could move on constructively."

"What happened? What did we learn?" he asked. "We learned that we must keep the focus on the end and the prize, and the prize is the professional issues facing this district -- not only here in Westwood -- but everywhere."

"We now need to have our doors open. We need to have our phones open. We need to become involved on a day-to-day basis and a week-to-week basis in solving not only the small problems of management relationships regarding the contract and teachers, but also the bigger concern of taking care of the school district's needs -- improving instruction, improving instruction, improving instruction," he finally concluded.

The Westwood Teachers' Alliance and School Committee, as a result of a number of positive forces coming together, agreed to establish the community's first mandatory Professional Development Academy in the district and finalized all contractual details in October 1998. It was agreed that the Academy would provide all teachers in Westwood with increased knowledge, skills, and renewal, in order to improve student learning. The Academy, in addition, would endeavor to promote inquiry, discourse, networking, and collaboration.

Through positive negotiations, the superintendent and the union agreed to work collaboratively to develop and implement the following elements of the Academy:

Governance - The Academy is to be organized and managed by a teacher who is either on sabbatical or receives one-half of his/her work schedule as released time. It is to be governed by an Academy member, a member of the teacher's union, a parent, the superintendent or his designee, and the teachers' union president or his designee.

Academy Trainers - Academy trainers may include Westwood teachers themselves who share expertise with colleagues, outside professionals, or college or university professionals.

Required Training -- As part of the Academy program, each Westwood teacher must engage in a minimum of eighteen (18) hours of training in the first year of the program and thirty hours (30) per year thereafter, one-third of which must be in technology or related fields.

The Academy took shape; it was fortuitous that the vice-president of the Westwood Teachers' Alliance, who played a central role in developing its concept, was its first director. His selection was, to some extent, controversial in that some members of the teachers' union voiced opinions that this choice was in effect pre-determined and, ironically, that the superintendent, school committee, and union were working too closely together. My selection of the academy's new director was based on a unanimous recommendation of the Academy's board of directors and was also unanimously approved by the Westwood School Committee.

In recommending the appointment of the vice-president of the teachers' union as the Academy's director, I knew I was risking criticism since other members of the teachers' union had applied for the position and were skeptical about adding a member of the union's leadership to the administrative team. His appointment, however, was the right choice and in the best interest of students.

To new and prospective school administrators, it must be emphasized that there will almost always be complaints no matter what course of action one takes. It is essential, however, to try to anticipate when possible both the short- and long-term negative reactions to decisions and have necessary information available to diffuse criticism. In short, one must be aware of the political implications of the decisions one makes.

In any given community, the ground rules will be different, but the superintendent must learn the rules of political engagement, in most cases, abide by them, and when necessary, find ways to renegotiate them. As I worked to negotiate and implement the professional development concept in Westwood, I thought that my most difficult challenges would involve engaging school committee and union leadership. What I did not anticipate, however, was the need to promote the product to individual teachers. The superintendent must recognize that the political forces he/she must address are not those that would normally be anticipated. The selection of the teachers' union vice-president as the Academy's first director helped to compensate for this lack of foresight on my part.

With the inception of the Academy concept, the director indicated that "having the leadership on board" did not necessarily mean that all members of the union were "on board." Much more work had to be done. One of the most effective early actions taken to ensure the Academy's success was to meet with each of the 330 faculty members to communicate goals and objectives. Seeking faculty input on new projects is normal. The director stressed the fact that the Academy needed the superintendent's active support. Accordingly, the superintendent met with each school faculty. These meetings went a long way to set the tone for the success of the Professional Development Academy.

Chapter 5

Managing The Superintendent's Time
Or
When The Manager Meets The Monkey

The time demands of a superintendent of schools' workload can be frenetic. Most superintendents, on any given day, have scheduled administrative staff meetings, meetings with complaining parents, student discipline hearings, meetings with outside consultants, and professional development activities. Add to this schedule unanticipated calls from school committee members with politically charged concerns, evening school committee meetings, and involvement with community organizations; and it is easy to understand how the demands of the superintendency can be overwhelming.

Personal survival often requires that superintendents devise time management strategies that allow for a workable mix of work, family, and leisure time. Failure to do so can result in an ineffective superintendency. The task of time management, in many ways, is a complicated one for most superintendents and must often be negotiated with school board members. For prospective superintendents, it is crucial to define one's priorities and stand by them. It is sometimes necessary to change and renegotiate. The superintendent's role, as stated earlier, is quasi-political, but it is also indeed, personal. One needs to find balance between the two.

Robert L. DeBruyn, editor of a publication I often find helpful, *Superintendents Only,* humorously observes, "Any time two or more superintendents get together and talk shop, they naturally gravitate to two subjects: who has the worst board--and who works the most sixteen-hour days."

It is shocking, as he goes on to note, how many superintendents publicly boast about the crazy hours they work. They work on weekends, neglect their families, and often refuse to take vacations. But those who think they are indispensable die right along with everyone else, though usually a little sooner.

I certainly agree with DeBruyn and suggest to the reader that working eighty-hour weeks will eventually result in diminishing returns and the loss of energy, drive, and interest.

It is the superintendent's responsibility not only to fulfill basic work functions, but also to maintain a professional role that is positive, energetic, and motivational. Overwork and poor time management can sometimes make these responsibilities difficult to fulfill.

There is, obviously, no easy or foolproof system to achieve the sense of desired control and balance. The best advice I have encountered comes from the work of William Oncken, Jr., and Donald L. Wass in "Management Time: Who's Got the Monkey?" (Harvard Business Review -- November-December, 1974). Their thoughts on time management for leaders of business and public organizations, though some twenty-five years old, continue to be both thought-provoking and effective. At the time of the Harvard article, Oncken was Chairman of the Board and Wass was president of the William Oncken Company of Texas, a management consulting firm. Their work addresses the basic question, "Why is it managers are typically running out of time?" The title of their article, "Management Time: Who's Got the Monkey," is an analogy that underscores the value of assigning and delegating responsibilities in an organization.

Oncken and Wass specifically deal with three different kinds of management time. Just to recognize these different types of time is a positive start for the new superintendent on the path to productive time management.

These definitions of time include the following:

Boss-imposed time -- time to accomplish activities, which the boss (in this case, the school board) requires, and which the manager cannot disregard without direct and swift penalty.

System-imposed time -- time to accommodate requests of the manager for active peer support, where assistance must be provided lest there be penalties, though not always direct or swift.

Self-imposed time -- time to do those tasks which the manager originates or agrees to do himself. Such self-imposed time is then usually subdivided in two ways. Time that will be taken by subordinates, which is termed "subordinate-imposed time," and finally, "discretionary time" which will be the manager's own to use as he or she desires.

The basic objective of good managers, according to Oncken and Wass, is to maximize their availability of self-imposed discretionary time and minimize the use of "subordinate-imposed" time. This motivation while seemingly selfish, is in fact, most often in the best interests of an organization in that it frees the manager to continue developing his or her long-term vision and chart future courses of action. The implicit assumption is that organizations that are not continuously evolving in new ways will be doomed to stagnation, failure, or extinction. Managers in most organizations spend much more subordinate-imposed time than they even faintly realize. Oncken and Wass illustrate this point through their use of their "Who's got the monkey" analogy. They state,

"Let us imagine that a manager is walking down the hall (in this case a school) and that he notices one of his subordinates, Mr. A., coming up the hallway. When

the manager and Mr. A. are abreast of one another, Mr. A. greets the manager with the statement, 'Good Morning. By the way, we've got a problem. You see . . .'"

As Mr. A. continues, the manager recognizes in the problem the same two characteristics common to all problems the manager's subordinates bring to his attention. Namely, the manager knows (a) enough to get involved, but (b) not enough to make the on the spot decision expected of him. The manager eventually says, "So glad you brought this up. I'm in a rush right now. Meanwhile, let me think about it and I'll let you know." Then the manager and Mr. A. part company.

Oncken and Wass, in analyzing this vignette, ask the question as to whose back was the problem or "monkey" on first. Obviously, Mr. A. After they parted, on whose back was it? The manager's. Subordinate-imposed time began the moment the monkey successfully executed a leap from the back of a subordinate to the manager's and would not end until the monkey was returned to its original owner for care and feeding.

According to Oncken and Wass, in accepting the monkey or taking responsibility to solve the problem, the manager has voluntarily assumed a position subordinate to his subordinate. That is, he has allowed Mr. A. to make him his subordinate by doing two things a subordinate is generally expected to do for his boss. The manager has accepted a responsibility, and the manager has promised a progress report.

Oncken and Wass cite many similar examples. Two of them follow.

In concluding a working conference with another subordinate, Mr. B., the manager's parting words are, "Fine. Send me a memo on that. Put your description of the problem in writing."

As Oncken and Wass indicate, at first glance, it now seems that the monkey is on the subordinate's back.

Subsequently, however, Mr. B. dutifully writes the requested memo and sends it to the manager. Whose move is it now? The manager's. If he does not make that move soon, he will get a follow-up memo from the subordinate. The longer the manager delays, the more frustrated the subordinate will become and the more guilty the manager will feel. An alternative initial course of action for the manager would have been to tell the subordinate to commit to writing his suggestions as how to solve the problem rather than to describe it.

This scenario is replayed with another subordinate, Mr. D., who has been transferred from another part of the company in order to launch a newly created business venture. The manager tells him that they should get together soon to hammer out a set objective for his new job, and that, "I will draw up an initial draft for discussion with you."

In analyzing this situation, Oncken and Wass point out that the subordinate has the new job, by formal assignment, and the full responsibility, by formal delegation, but the manager has the next move. Until he makes it, he will have the monkey, and the subordinate will be immobilized.

These situations occur because in each instance the manager and the subordinate assume at the outset, wittingly or unwittingly, that the concerns under consideration are joint problems.

The manager failed to assume his responsibility to delegate. Rather than offer to get together with Mr. D. to hammer out objections, for example, he should have directed Mr. D. to draft the objectives and then meet to review them. Subsequently, the manager would then suggest changes to the draft that Mr. D. would then implement.

In conclusion, Oncken and Wass emphasize that there are five degrees of initiatives that members of an organization may take. These include the options: (1) wait until told (lowest initiative); (2) ask what to do; (3) recommend, then take resulting action; (4) act, but advise at once; and (5) act, then routinely report (highest initiative.)

Clearly, the manager should be professional enough not to indulge in initiatives 1 and 2. A manager who uses initiative 1 has no control. He thereby forfeits any right to complain about what he is told to do or when he is told to do it. The manager who uses initiative 2 has control over timing but not content. Initiatives 3, 4, and 5 leave the manager in control of both, with the greatest control being at level 5.

The manager's job, in relation to his subordinate's initiative, is twofold; first, to forego the use of initiatives 1 and 2, thus giving his subordinates no choice but to learn and master; and second, to see that for each problem leaving his office, there is an agreed-upon level of initiative on the part of staff assigned to it.

The first order of business to accomplish these objectives is for the manager to increase his discretionary time by eliminating subordinate-imposed time. The second is for him to use a portion of his newly found discretionary time to see to it that each of his subordinates possesses initiative that is in fact taken. The third is for the manager to use another portion of increased discretionary time to control the timing and content of both boss-imposed and system-imposed time.

The result of all this is that the manager's leverage, will increase, which, in time, will enable him to multiply, without theoretical limit, the value of each hour that he spends in managing time.

Based on my experience, one of the first and most important challenges for a new superintendent is to understand the need to obtain and maintain discretionary time and mutually define with one's school committee both the boss-imposed and system-imposed demands on the superintendent's time. Failure to agree on a mutually acceptable definition of boss-imposed time is a certain path to failure for a superintendent.

Often when a new superintendent enters a district, public and school board expectations for change and improvement are unrealistically high as is their understanding of the superintendent's limited ability to introduce change immediately and unilaterally.

As a new superintendent recognizes and attempts to negotiate a more realistic definition of the use of time, one of the most effective approaches is to attempt to agree on a few of the major issues that should be a central focus in working with school committee members.

When I came to Westwood, a central concern of the school committee involved the deployment of administrative staff. This concern related to site-based issues discussed earlier and the use of administrative time and resources. Previous school committees had begun a process of decentralizing administrative control of the district. This process was evidenced by its restructuring of central office administration.

The central office leadership team prior to this restructuring included the Superintendent, the Special Education Director, Director of Administration, a Curriculum Director, and a Director of Compensatory Education who was responsible for remedial reading, language arts, and English-as-a-Second-Language programs. When the Curriculum Director and Director of Compensatory Programs retired in the mid-1990's, these vacant positions were eliminated. The school committee, utilizing budgeted salaries for these positions, then moved to hire two assistant principals at the elementary level, thus providing principals with assistant principals at each of the community's three largest elementary schools. The thinking at the time was that a bolstering of administration at the school-based level would facilitate a smooth and more productive transition to the district's site-based approach to school improvement.

Based on my experience in Wellton, I had a different approach in mind. During my tenure there, I observed a need for alignment and coordination of curricula, especially at the elementary level. The need for such coordination, to some extent, was based on high migration patterns of students within the city. With one of the highest percentages of rental properties in the state, families in the community would often move from one section of the city to another, seeking improvements in their rented apartments.

On numerous occasions, parents of elementary school children complained that their children were lost in their new school. Others inquired, "Why don't they teach the same thing in one third grade at one school as they do in another?" Such questions were difficult for a central office administrator to answer. Related issues are also often ignored when students' performance levels in communities with high migration rates are compared with their counterparts in more stable affluent communities.

I am somewhat skeptical about the benefits of a pure site-based management model without a strong district-wide focus on strategic planning, goal setting, and alignment of school-based plans. Site-based management in its purest form places decision making and problem solving into the hands of teachers and staff -- those closest to the students. Concepts that I must agree with.

A recent research project conducted by Harold Wenglinsky and funded by the National Science Foundation (NSF) and the Educational Testing Service (ETS), however, indicates that some of the most clearly documented positive effects on student achievement have been the result of central office plans and interventions.

Wenglinsky, in *When Money Matters*, describes the unfolding saga of ongoing legal battles over school finance. Utilizing National Assessment of Educational Progress (NAEP) data, he traces the effects of different types of expenditures and school improvement interventions on student achievement. Types of expenditures involved in his analysis include level of financial investment in instruction, central office, principal's office, and capital outlays. His data is also adjusted for cost differences by district and state by using a teacher cost index produced by the National Center for Education Statistics.

Wenglinsky's findings are indeed interesting and provocative, must reading for any new or prospective superintendent. As background to his research, Wenglinsky notes that policy makers have traditionally been divided in their views on the proper course to follow in school finance, time and resource allocation. Some argue for a traditional approach and think that more money needs to be spent to reduce disparities between rich and poor districts. Others suggest raising spending levels in poor school districts above those in affluent ones to compensate for past inequities. From an opposing perspective, still others argue for a "productivity" approach and point to research that has shown that significant increases in spending and reductions of inequalities have not netted the increases expected in achievement.

The recent productivity approach has also emphasized the need for low-achieving school districts to cut wasteful spending and to invest resources in those areas most conducive to raising student achievement. The productivity approach, in addition, emphasizes that less money should be spent on district-level bureaucracy, and school principals should have increased budget discretion. According to this view, in its most basic form, the superintendent's office (according to Wenglinsky) is typically a "sink of waste, fraud, and abuse and viewed as creating obstacles for principals who want to run their school innovatively."

Wenglinsky's findings indicate otherwise. Utilizing advanced multivariate techniques to produce flow charts for fourth and eighth graders to determine how dollars and resources influence student achievement as measured by the NAEP, Wenglinsky found that expenditures can affect student outcomes in a two-step process for fourth graders and a three-step process for eighth graders.

Fourth grade findings:

Step 1: Increased expenditures on instruction and school district administration increase teacher-student ratios.

Step 2: Increased teacher-student ratios raise average achievement in mathematics.

Eighth grade findings:

Step 1: Increased expenditures on instruction and school district administration increase teacher-student ratios.

Step 2: Increased teacher-student ratios reduce problem behaviors and improve the social environment of the school.

Step 3: A lack of problem behaviors among students and a positive social environment raise average achievement in mathematics.

In addition, this study found that variations in other expenditures and resources were not associated with variations in achievement. The following illustrate this conclusion:

1. Capital outlays (spending on facility construction and maintenance)
2. School level (principal's office) administration
3. Teacher education levels.

Wenglinsky's study, in summary, provides some support for the productivity perspective and some support for the traditional perspective on school finance. It supports the notion among productivity researchers and policy makers that some dollars matter more than others. It also finds, interestingly, that some traditional spending practices of school districts, e.g. spending for teacher-to-student ratios and central office administration, are conducive to academic achievement.

As Wenglinsky concludes, his findings have significant policy implications for superintendents. While many critics of public education are concerned with bloated administrative bureaucracies in local school districts, his findings ironically suggest that a significant commitment to central office administration is associated with more money being spent on smaller classes. In addition, Wenglinsky also notes these same findings support the notion that while principals may be better positioned than central office staff to make instructional and personnel decisions, some budgetary decisions may be better left to the superintendent.

Buttressed in part by Wenglinsky's research, as I approached the administrative restructuring process in Westwood, I convinced the committee not to fill assistant principal positions at the elementary level and instead to utilize funds budgeted for these positions to hire additional central office staff to lead the curriculum improvement process.

Fortunately, two assistant principal vacancies occurred, which I replaced with two newly created positions. The first position was designated Mathematics Standards Implementation Specialist and the second, School Improvement Leader. The first position was filled by a veteran Westwood teacher with national teacher training experience. He stepped into a central office role. The second was filled by Carol Jones, an elementary principal with a statewide reputation for leading school improvement initiatives.

More time will certainly be needed to evaluate the effectiveness of my restructuring effort. There are, however, indications that it is already having the desired effect. The Math Standards Implementation Specialist is heavily involved in the Professional Development Academy. The School Improvement Leader has been well accepted by staff and is working productively with the assistant superintendent on realigning the curriculum.

I must admit that it is difficult to assess the impact of not filling the elementary school assistant principal positions. Again, however, indications seem positive. One school principal was having difficulty dealing with the increased number of disciplinary referrals. This problem was resolved by providing her with a disciplinary aide at one-fourth the cost of an assistant principal.

From a time and resource management perspective, I believe the changes I instituted were essential. The overall responsibilities of the superintendent and his assistant preclude their exclusive involvement in curriculum improvement needs. The resulting changes involved clear delegation of authority, which I believe is crucial to the success of a superintendent.

The research of Oncken and Wass indicates that it is the superintendent's or manager's job to enlarge his discretionary time and use a portion of it to assure that each of his subordinates possesses initiative and then to assure that initiative is in fact taken. Through implementation of my administrative restructuring plan, I believe this maxim was adhered to.

Chapter 6

Interscholastic Athletics/ Extracurricular Activities and Academic Support Programs

---

Some may ask why devote a chapter to interscholastic sports, extracurricular activities and support programs, when so many other issues may be more important to improving schools. The simple answer is that overseeing these programs is one of the most controversial, time-consuming, and difficult aspects of the superintendent's job.

Westwood has 26 sports teams ranging from traditional programs in baseball, basketball, and football to girls' gymnastics, volleyball, and field hockey. The 1999 high school athletic budget totaled $331,000 and served 196 student athletes or 20% of the total student population from grades nine through twelve.

The budget for non-athletic student activities, in contrast, totaled $57,800 and included funding for eighteen faculty advisors.   Related activities included traditional club programs such as: art, French, Italian, and music, student council, and honor societies. The funding gap between athletic programs and other student activities speaks much about both society's priorities and those of the community.

From a societal point of view, it is obvious that athletics and especially professional sports have assumed a large role in influencing children's attitudes, often in negative ways. The enormous salaries of professional athletes, their oftentimes negative behavior in terms of substance abuse, and their frequent displays of unprofessional conduct during games and events send negative messages to highly impressionable students.

Perhaps the greatest negative impact of professional sports in the United States is on the increasing number of students, especially in larger, poorer urban communities, who believe that athletics is a sure path to financial success since these students neglect to prepare for more likely careers.

Bill Reynolds, in his recent book, *Glory Days--On Sports, Men and Dreams That Don't Die*, describes the inadequate high school schedule of many student athletes in the U.S. as "a course load that is not particularly overpowering without the rigors of pre-college math, science, or a foreign language."

In November 1998, the National Collegiate Athletic Association (NCAA) released the graduation rates of Division 1-A and 1-AA athletes who were freshmen in 1991 and who had graduated by August

1997.   The following chart illustrates how the 1998 top ten college football teams fared.   The data support Reynolds's view.

Student athletes, in general, and football players, in particular, were reported to have graduation rates lower than those of non-athletes as a whole.   While certainly not reflective of the graduation rate for all student athletes, the results of these "top ten" schools contribute to the potentially destructive influence "big time" college sports may have on career decisions made by high school students.

	Division 1-A Football College Graduation Rates		
	Players	Student-Athletes	Student Body
1. Tennessee	11%	37%	56%
2. Kansas State	35%	43%	45%
3. UCLA	65%	63%	79%
4. Florida	20%	39%	64%
5. Florida State	63%	61%	65%
6. Texas A & M	43%	52%	69%
7. Ohio State	35%	54%	57%
8. Wisconsin	63%	60%	73%
9. Arizona	56%	54%	52%
10. Arkansas	14%	29%	42%

Research by the Center for the Study of Sports in Society at Northeastern (1998) indicates that an incredible number (66%) of African American seventh and eighth graders from the twenty largest urban areas in America believe they will become professional athletes.   This, despite the overwhelming odds, for example, that only one high school student in 50,000 will play in the National Basketball Association.   Athletics certainly can and do have a positive place in schools and society at large. The negatives, however, often seem to outweigh the positives as too many students seem to imitate the inflated egotistic behavior of their professional role models.

A recent incident in Rhode Island's Valley Regional School District, reveals a pattern of negative behavior on the part of students, coaches, and parents that is all too common.

Prior to the Valley Chargers' last regular season game of 1998, with its opponent at the field and ready to compete, they refused to play. The team's decision not to play stemmed from an incident on the Friday prior to the scheduled Tuesday match against one of Valley's archrivals.   That two-to-two contest ended with one player from each team tangling after the final whistle. A Valley player, in addition, reportedly spat at an opposing player, and a Valley fan came out of the stands, screaming, and threatening one of the opposing coaches.

The Valley coach, as a result, suspended two of his players for the ensuing Tuesday game. The other Valley players, however, felt that the suspensions were unfair and boycotted the Tuesday game even though they knew their actions would affect the playoff standings of other teams in their division.

The players' behavior presented a significant challenge to Valley's principal, Tom Raine. He reacted quickly and positively.   Raine indicated that he was shocked when he had heard what happened in a follow-up newspaper interview and stated, "The decision by those players not to participate in a school game altered the league standings and the playoff format. The actions of any team to pick and choose to play when committed to a league game is totally unacceptable." After much thought, he decided to end the Valley boys' soccer season and not participate in the playoffs.

Raine's decision was difficult to accept by many, but was a sound one. Case closed. The lesson for prospective administrators, however, becomes clear when one hears of the reactions of Valley's players, parents, and fellow coaches to Raine's decision.

Subsequent to his decision, Raine met with his team and coaching staff to explain his view. He reported that they were stunned. "They just don't get it. Some of them were running their mouths off at me." Raine lamented, "They want to blame every one else for their actions. I believe that they have to understand that there are consequences to pay for those actions."

Thomas Smith, director of Rhode Island's Interscholastic League, stated, "The Valley program has been out of control for the last couple of years. The team has been the target of numerous complaints of unsportsmanlike conduct this season; too many, many yellow-card and red-card violations. The problem has not only been with the players but the parents as well."

Incidents like the Valley episode indicate why I have found decisions regarding school sports among the most difficult and controversial.

The highest attendance at a school committee meeting during my tenure in Wellton focused on a debate between school department coaches and athletes on one side, and coaches and parents of non-school athletes on the other side, regarding use of the city's athletic fields. In all, over one hundred people represented each group with police presence necessary to retain order. Use of the community's athletic facilities drew more community interest than any other education-related issue in Wellton.

On many occasions, members of the Westwood School Committee have shared with me the volatile nature of school sports in the community in a historical context and emphasized how related tensions have tended to dominate the political landscape of school affairs in the town.

These tensions were clearly visible in an incident involving the recent hiring of a new varsity football coach. As noted in a *Providence Journal* account (May 1999), when Westwood High School freshman football coach Jim Jones was passed over for promotion to varsity coach, a number of student athletes in Westwood experienced the unpleasant side of school sports.

A week after the Westwood School Committee appointed the varsity coach, the freshman coach wrote a heartfelt letter to the local newspaper voicing some concern over the hiring process. Subsequently, while serving as the high school's golf coach, he was confronted by the uncle of the successful candidate. Words were exchanged and a shoving match allegedly occurred in front of the golf team.

Although the confrontation was brief and produced no injuries, it certainly underscored the passion townspeople bring to the fortunes of the home team.

Another of the most controversial school sports issue I faced in Westwood involved debate over the school committee's right to terminate tenure for the school district's coaches. The debate focused on the fact that as a result of new contract provisions, coaches would become employees "at will" for the school district.

While I was speaking with Westwood School Committee Chairperson Tom Silva about this issue, he emphasized that the committee had sought the provision to allow more flexibility in the coaches' hiring process and also thought the provision could become a wedge that might someday be used to address the issue of lifetime teacher tenure.

As background to the current discussion, it should be noted that Rhode Island's law regarding teacher tenure is among the strongest in the country and had, up to this time, been applied to coaches in Westwood. Chapter 16-13-2 of the General Laws of Rhode Island states, "Teaching service shall be on the basis of an annual contract, except as hereinafter provided, and the contract shall be deemed to be continuous unless the governing body of the schools shall notify the teacher in writing on or before March 1 that the contract for the ensuing year will not be renewed; provided, however, that a teacher, upon request, shall be furnished a statement of cause for dismissal or nonrenewal of his or her contract by the school committee; provided further, that whenever any contract is not renewed, or the teacher is dismissed, the teacher shall be entitled to a hearing and appeal pursuant to the procedure set forth in 16-13-4."

Further, Chapter 16-13-3 indicates that three successive annual contracts shall be considered evidence of satisfactory teaching and that teachers who have given satisfactory service for three years shall be considered in continuing service. No such teacher shall be dismissed except for good and just cause. In effect, then, Chapter 16 provides Rhode Island teachers with lifetime tenure subsequent to three years of positive continuous service.

To terminate a teacher, according to Rhode Island's General Laws, school committees must provide a statement of cause to the teacher and accord that teacher a public hearing. Any teacher aggrieved by the decision of the school board shall have a right of appeal to the State Department of Elementary and Secondary Education and shall have the right of further appeal to the Superior Court. Rhode Island law is also clear with regard to administrators' rights to job security. According to 16-12-1.2.1, an administrator shall only be terminated for just cause including, but not limited to, declining enrollment or consolidation.

Throughout their careers, public school athletic coaches in Westwood and in many other communities throughout the country have held similar tenure rights to their positions and established long and storied careers. The Westwood School Committee, by winning at the arbitration table, however, had changed the rules of the game for the process of selecting coaches. As one school committee member confided to me, "I am really surprised that we won; now watch the firestorm when we attempt to implement this thing." The school committee member was right. During my work in Westwood, this one issue resulted in more telephone calls, discussions with attorneys, and rancorous meetings with staff, than any other. Part of the concern was based especially on existing provisions in the teachers' contract related to the posting of positions for appointment and/or reappointment.

After winning the arbitrator's decision, the Westwood School Committee was still faced with negotiating and agreeing upon language as to how the arbitrator's ruling regarding athletic coaches could be implemented. The agreement reached with the teachers' union stated:

"All coaches shall be subject to reappointment or appointment for a three (3) year term. Qualifications as determined by the school committee being equal, bargaining unit members shall be given preference. It shall not be a prerequisite to coach a Westwood school team or that the appointee be an actively employed teacher of the Westwood School System." (Contract between the Westwood School Committee and Westwood Teachers' Alliance 1998-2000 -- Article 36.) This agreement meant in effect that not only would incumbent coaches be subject to reappointment, but it also stipulated that their positions would be open to outside applicants.

During the first phases of implementing this contract language, fourteen coaching positions were advertised in local and statewide newspapers. Protests by incumbent coaches were indeed significant. One of the coaches' first tactics was to challenge the legality of the school committee's and their own union's agreement. During my five years as an assistant superintendent or superintendent, this was the first time I had encountered such questioning of union actions by their own membership.

Prior to the matter coming to court, Westwood's attorney tried to stem this round of protest by citing a 1980 Rhode Island Commissioner of Education's decision -- Milman vs. the Barrington School Committee.

This decision concerned Mr. Milman's dismissal as a basketball and tennis coach at Barrington High School. After testimony was taken, the Commissioner noted the following facts:

1.   The appellant was employed at Barrington High School as the basketball coach for the 1978-79 and

1979-80 basketball seasons and as the tennis coach for the 1979 tennis season.

2.   The appellant was a teacher in the North Providence, Rhode Island, School System during the time he was employed as a coach at Barrington High School.

3.   The appellant was not rehired as the basketball coach for the 1980-81 basketball season nor as the tennis coach for the 1980 tennis season.

4.   There was no written contract covering the appellant's services as a coach at Barrington High School.

The Commissioner, having considered these facts, ruled that the appellant had no promise of, or legitimate claim of entitlement to, continued employment as a coach beyond the time he was so employed in Barrington. In other words, the Commissioner ruled the coach was deprived of no property interest and therefore had no constitutional or statutory basis to claim any greater degree of due process than he received. The Commissioner, in this regard, also cited the following language from the decision of the United States Court of Appeals for the First Circuit in *Ventetuolo v. Burke*, 596 F.2d 476, 480.

"To have a property interest that is constitutionally protected by due process, appellant must have had a legitimate claim of entitlement to continued employment arising out of law. A unilateral expectation is not sufficient."

To most observers, the Commissioner's decision would seem clear and relevant to the Westwood coaches' position. While one might appreciate the coaches' complaints or be sympathetic to them, they certainly did not have basis in terms of the teachers' union contract with the Westwood School Committee or Rhode Island law. The coaches' protests, however, continued as they complained to school committee members, fellow teachers, parents' groups, and anyone else in the community who would listen.

Frustrated with their own union leadership who agreed with the applicability of the Milman v. Barrington decision to their situation, the coaches then took the further step of directing a list of fourteen questions to me. A sample of the coaches' questions and my responses to them are reprinted below and convey the coaches' deep sense of frustration and, I believe, continued lack of understanding of the related contract agreement between the Westwood Teachers' Alliance and the School Committee.

1.   Q.   **What is the actual status of winter coaches since our positions, as of October 11, 1998, were identified as vacant in the *Providence Sunday Journal*?**

      A.   In accord with Article 36 of the Westwood Teachers' Alliance contract, these positions are now up for reappointment.

2.   Q.   **Who is responsible for the procedure being used to implement Article 36? What were the reasons for choosing this procedure?**

A.   The procedure that was used is required by
       Article 7 Section A Subsection 1 of the
       contract. This process requires that all new
       or vacant positions be posted.

3. Q.   **There is in place a school department
           procedure for reappointment. It is the
           procedure used to reappoint the
           superintendent, assistant superintendent,
           principals, vice-principals, etc. These
           positions are not vacated when the
           contract expires and then posted in the
           paper to see if any other candidates are
           available. Instead, job performance,
           evaluations, etc. are used and the person is
           reappointed. Yet, for a part-time coaching
           position, which has far less impact, a
           major procedure has been created? Why?**

    A.   The other non-coaching positions you
           referenced are not governed by the
           Westwood School Committee contract
           agreement with the Westwood Teachers'
           Alliance. In addition, the positions you
           referenced such as superintendent, assistant
           superintendent, and principals are
           governed by R.I. General Law Title 16
           regarding the right of incumbents in these
           positions to not be terminated without just
           cause. Coaches, on the other hand, "serve
           at the pleasure" of their employer. The
           principle was clearly spelled out in a
           Commissioner of Education decision in the

case of Jeffrey A. Milman vs. the Barrington School Committee, November 7, 1980. In this decision, the Commissioner refers to other court decisions including a United States Court of Appeals case and previous decisions of the Commissioner, which established the principle that coaches have a unilateral expectation, which is not a property interest that is constitutionally protected by due process and coaches do not have a legitimate claim or entitlement to continue in employment arising out of Rhode Island law as do teachers and administrators.

4.   Q.   **Why was the Athletic Director not part of the planning of this new procedure? He is, after all, the head of the department. Is this not a bypass of the chain of command?**

      A.   The system and new procedures have been discussed on numerous occasions with the Athletic Director, going back as far as the last school year.

5.   Q.   **Are any other school programs, academic departments, or groups being MICRO managed to this level? If so, what are they?**

      A.   As mentioned, school athletic programs are being "managed" in accord with the contract between the Westwood Teachers'

Alliance and the Westwood School Committee. It is interesting to note also that we have had the pleasure of implementing other new and productive management practices such as the initiation of a voting process to determine department chairs as opposed to simply selecting them based on past experience or seniority.

6.   Q.   **Legal issues aside, coaches have tried to be part of the process to include taking the lead in the development of a coaches' evaluation program, yet the union and the administration chose to leave the coaches out of the most important aspect. Why?**

      A.   I certainly cannot speak on behalf of the Westwood Teachers' Alliance (union). I can, however, state that the administration has worked cooperatively with your union, your legal representatives, to implement this new coaching reappointment procedure. It is my understanding that coaches did indeed have input into the evaluation process. This input took place between teacher representatives on the Teacher Evaluation Committee (TEC) and the Coaches' Association.

7.   Q.   **Did anyone bother to consider the repercussion this experience has had on the coaches who have for <u>years</u> devoted time, money, personal family time, and**

other sacrifices to help student athletes of Westwood be successful, both on and off the athletic field and what an insult it has been to us to be treated in this manner?

A.   Yes.

Having responded to the questions of the coaches in a straightforward manner, I mistakenly thought that related issues would be resolved. An incident that took place during a subsequent interview of one of our coaches who was facing the reappointment process clearly suggested otherwise.

My office had formed an interview committee of a school committee member, administrators, parents, and students to interview coaches in order to implement the reappointment process. One veteran hockey coach chose to use this forum to read a written statement expressing his frustration about the reappointment process. In addition, when asked what he found to be positive about the high school sports programs, he responded that before the new coaches' evaluation and reappointment process, "Everything," and "Now I see only negative."

The school committee member on the interview committee and one of the parents immediately contacted me the next morning to express their dissatisfaction and disappointment with the coach's behavior and stated, "He should not be allowed to coach in this school district." The majority of members of the committee seemed to share this frustration, but, nevertheless, recommended the coach for reappointment. I personally was angry and took the coach's action as an affront to my authority.

In discussing the issue with other members of the school committee, it became apparent that I could marshal enough votes not to reappoint the veteran coach and to select an outside candidate.

Based on conversations with other administrators and teachers, however, it was also clear that this would not be in the best interest of the student athletes in that the veteran coach was still probably the best candidate for this position.   This dilemma, while not insurmountable, was a serious one for a superintendent. If I left the coach's comments unaddressed, I thought I would leave a challenge to my authority unaddressed; if I chose not to reappoint the coach, I would be hurting students.

My solution was to call a meeting with the coach and demand that he provide a written apology to the interview committee. I informed him, in addition, that if he did not provide the apology, I could not, in good conscience, recommend his reappointment, in that his choice of the interview forum to vent his frustration over the reappointment process was indicative of poor judgment that might be reflective of his decision making relative to student athletes.

While this would seem to be a simple and rational solution to the problem on my part, such a course of action was not without risk. The coach could have called my bluff, I would have been forced not to recommend his appointment, and, for at least the short term, there would have been no winners. The coach would not be reappointed, the student athletes would suffer, and I, as superintendent, would likely be facing a long, public grievance process as the coach sought reinstatement.

We were all fortunate.   The coach, Mr. Ken Harvard, decided to admit he was wrong and provided the letter of apology to the committee. In addition, a constructive discussion clarified the reappointment process, which, in turn, defined the relative positions of both parties.

As superintendents consider other issues related to interscholastic sports, it is important that they be viewed within the more general context of student activities, the way students spend their discretionary time, and issues regarding the potential benefits of extended school day programs. Policy makers at the national, state, and local levels have been focusing increasingly on related topics, and the challenges for new superintendents are significant as they attempt to keep the emphasis on student achievement.

The news, according to recent research, is both good and bad (University of Michigan's Institute for Social Research [1998]). Interestingly, America's children today spend less time watching television than they did in the early 1980's and spend more time engaged in sports and slightly more on school work.

Among the most striking changes is the increase in the time spent at school, up by an average of more than 90 minutes weekly since 1981. According to the University of Michigan study, this is happening not because academic school days are longer, but because more children are in pre-school and before- and after-school child-care programs as a result of an increase of mothers in the labor force.

The study found that children's free time left after going to school, eating, and sleeping has decreased from forty percent of a child's day in 1981 to 25 percent in 1997. After collecting minute-by-minute time diaries from the families of 3,600 children, researchers in the Michigan study led by Sandra L. Hofferth, were able to describe in detail how a typical child's week plays out, from the average of 74 hours of sleeping to the nine hours spent eating.

Children, overall, average about 90 minutes of television viewing on weekdays, down from two hours in 1981. Television, however, still occupies far more of a child's time than does homework or reading.

Average study time on weekdays has gone up for boys, from fourteen minutes to twenty-one minutes, since the early 1980's. For girls, the figure has gone from nineteen minutes to twenty-two minutes. Reading at home, even for 12-year olds, occupies less than an hour and a half each week, no more than in 1981. This is not good news.

Boys on average spend twice as much time as girls playing sports. The typical six-year old, for example, spends a half-hour each week on computers, while a twelve-year old spends an hour and twelve minutes.

Finally, researchers in the University of Michigan study note that the data shows that every hour spent reading at home each week translates into a half-point increase in achievement test scores, while each additional hour spent watching television decreases test scores by one-tenth of a point on tests where the mean score was 100.

Recognizing the apparent value of additional time on task and homework in 1994, the Boston School Committee raised the recommended amount of homework in that community by a half-hour, to 2-1/2 hours per night. According to a recent *Boston Globe* (November 10, 1998) survey, however, a majority of Boston high school students say they only receive an average of a half-hour to an hour of homework per night. In this regard, data from a 1996 Massachusetts

Department of Education study shows that the majority of Boston's tenth grade students report doing less than two hours of homework per night with 39% stating that they do one to two hours and 37% stating they do less than one hour. In related *Boston Globe* interviews, most principals, headmasters, and teachers say they constantly search for ways to instill the value of homework. They also point out, however, that many students say they have to do their classwork, but they do not have to do homework.

As Boston High School headmaster Thomas Hennessey observes, "A lot of kids have the mentality that if they pay attention in class and they do their classwork, that's it. But we can't give up."

Ironically, results from another study point in an opposite direction. A recent article by Etta Kralovec, the director of teachers at the College of the Atlantic in Miami, and John Buell, a columnist for the *Bangor Daily News* (*Boston Globe*, November 15, 1998), surprisingly emphasizes that much research does not show a consistent correlation between long hours spent doing homework and student performance.

As the authors indicate, research from the Massachusetts Department of Education suggests that there is a direct link between the socioeconomic status of a community and time spent on homework. A related research problem is whether or not homework makes good, motivated students or whether good, motivated students do a great deal of homework.

In her research at the College of the Atlantic, Kralovec found that extensive homework played a major role in determining school dropouts. In ethnographic interviews, Kralovec's research team asked students if there was a moment when they knew they were going to drop out of school. Kralovec indicates that these students' tales told the story of incomplete homework and an inability to fit homework into their lives.

According to Kralovec, when schools emphasize extensive homework and parents are overburdened with household chores, childcare, work schedules and overtime, young children often study alone at home. Frequently, exhausted parents, usually women, must help their children with homework late into the night.

To Kralovec, public education has long been the target of choice for social critics but schools often come to reflect the worst features of the society they were designed to improve. She cites the work of Bowles and Gintis, "Schooling in Capitalist America," where they argue that much of the structure of public education-- early tracking, rote instruction--can be explained in part as an effort to prepare students for the assembly line of the harshest corporate workplaces. In the process, schools reinforce a corporate order that underestimates its greatest assets--worker talent and imagination. Kralovec concludes that current school and homework practices will never encourage creative and self-directed workers and citizens. While seemingly radical, Kralovec's comments have important implications for school administrators.

Winerip (1999) makes similar points in tracing the historical route of the homework issue. As he notes, there is an assumption that the current trend to give more homework is a return to traditional values; however, this is not the case. Drawing on related research, he emphasizes that for much of this century, leading educators have deplored the practice of assigning homework at an early age.

As early as the 1890's, according to Gill and Schlossman, a muckraking doctor, Joseph Mayer Rice, attacked the homework "spelling grind," and stated, "Is it not our duty to save the child from the grind?"

Further, in 1900, Commissioner of Education William Torrey Harris testified before Congress that there should be no homework before age twelve. Furthermore, Winerip notes, "In the twenty years before World War I, the *Ladies' Home Journal* led a national crusade against homework. As a result, teachers wrote to thank the editor and expressed that they were afraid if they criticized mandatory homework practices, they would lose their jobs."

Winerip, in addition, emphasizes that newspapers like *The New York Times* editorialized against homework during the same time period, and in 1930, the American Child Health Association classified homework as a form of child labor. During the 1920's and 30's, New York City public schools banned homework until fourth grade, San Diego banned it through eighth grade, and Sacramento had a prohibition on elementary school homework for forty-five years, until 1961.

According to Winerip, however, whenever the nation has felt an external threat, educators have manned the barricades by piling on homework. Homework grew in popularity in the 1950's, after the Russians launched Sputnik, and continued in favor until the late 1960's, with the American economy in recession, the Japanese in ascent, and the publication of the study "A Nation At Risk," maintaining that our educational system was lagging behind other industrialized nations. Homework returned to fashion and has kept its popularity right through the global economy years.

As Winerip concludes his discussion of the homework controversy, he cites the comments of a veteran assistant superintendent of schools when asked during a recent interview whether she felt elementary students had too much homework in her district. "She said no, that it builds good study habits and discipline for future years. But if you talked to me in the 1970's, I'd have given you a different answer."

The University of Michigan study, Kralovec's research, and Winerip's commentary present two significant challenges to superintendents: First, assessing the impact of increasing homework and before- and after school programs. Second, implementing changes to improve related interventions when necessary.

In Westwood, I shared a priority with the school committee to explore before- and after-school programs in both recreational and academic areas.

During the next two years, we were able to implement breakfast programs and after-school academic tutorial programs in all schools, establish school/community partnerships at the middle and high school involving college students serving as role models and tutors to at-risk students, and finally, expand a middle school after-school recreational program so that it is now the largest in Rhode Island serving 35% of the 900 students at that facility.

As Westwood's superintendent, I must report, however, that we have little research to determine the impact of these programs. One of my goals for the next two years will be to implement a comprehensive evaluation assessment of these programs. A central problem, as with all types of education research, will be to evaluate interconnecting factors such as family income, level of education of parents, and other demographic characteristics in an attempt to identify any achievement differences between students who do and do not participate in auxiliary programs. In addition, making time, identifying resources to conduct research, and parent and student involvement will be issues to be addressed in the future. The benefits of this research make its completion a priority.

It has been clear for many years that programs providing social and academic support beyond the regular school day can enhance the achievement of at-risk students, especially in the elementary grades. It has also become apparent, however, that all intervention strategies are not clearly effective (Rand Corporation 1989). According to this study, it is especially important that supplementary tasks or support bear a clear relationship to the student's school curriculum and be sustained. Positive intervention programs need to involve parents, teachers, and students in their development and identify clear benchmarks for improved student achievement.

In *Waiting for a Miracle--Why Schools Can't Solve Our Problems--And How We Can*, James P. Comer, M.D., describes a number of productive and sustained support or youth development programs that may serve as models for other communities. One such program is St. HOPE Academy.

Kevin Johnson, a National Basketball Association All-Star, founded St. HOPE in 1989 in his old neighborhood, Oak Park, just south of Sacramento, California. HOPE stands for Help Our People Excel.

According to Comer, Oak Park is a depressed neighborhood where the median income of $14,732.00 is less than half that of Sacramento. Many of the program participants are influenced by gang and drug cultures, lack positive role models and guidance, and come from dysfunctional families.   The academy provides these students with opportunities for educational, cultural, and social experiences and expression. Forty-eight children, aged eight to thirteen, are in the program for one and a half hours each day of the school year after school, and all day during the summer, for individual tutoring, meals, workshops, club activities, and special programs. Qualifying students receive additional school guidance, SAT preparation, social counseling, and employment placement. Graduates of the program are then recruited to tutor and mentor younger children.   I agree with Comer when he argues, "The St. HOPE Academy is one that we all can learn from."

As new superintendents attempt to develop a framework for evaluating the suitability of new school improvement and/or before and after-school support programs, many useful suggestions are provided by Stringfield (1998.)   Stringfield, a principal research scientist at the Johns Hopkins University Center for the Social Organization of Schools, emphasizes that there is no shortage of programs that promise to turn around low-performing students and schools.   I highly recommend his summary of the best methods to evaluate their effectiveness. Stringfield, essentially, suggests that there are three basic questions every school system should consider as it contemplates replicating new intervention strategies.

First, are the goals and objectives of the program in line with the goals and objectives of the school district? He notes, "No matter how sound a program is, or how successful elsewhere, it will be a waste of everyone's time and effort if it is not designed to get your school or district where you want it to go."

Second, how strong is the research supporting the program's claims of success? For Stringfield, answering this question, which hinges on a number of technical issues, is likely to be the most daunting. Quoting Al Shanker, "None of us would use a medicine that had not been found to be safe and effective in rigorous research. Why should we expect anything less of the programs we hope will reform our schools?"

Third, given available funding and personnel, is a given plan practical? Stringfield concludes that a program might come with the best possible pedigree in terms of research design and prior success, but if the financial or human costs are beyond the resources of a school district, the design is of no real value.

As mentioned earlier, managing after-school, before-school, and adjunct programs and activities demand a great deal of a superintendent's time and energy. Introduction of new programs and activities should only be done with caution and without creating unrealistic expectations. When a new superintendent enters his or her school district, during the first few weeks or months, many staff and community members will suggest new programs and initiatives. The role of the new superintendent should be to base decisions regarding these suggestions in prior and ongoing research.

Chapter 7

Student Achievement Individual Versus Collective Responsibility

---

Recently, I became convinced that public educators must rethink their thinking concerning the relationship between competition and achievement. I have viewed schooling for most of my career within the context of sociological status attainment theory. Expressed in simple terms, I have always believed that effort in school, educational achievement, social status, and satisfaction in life were for the most part connected in a linear way and that the role of teachers, administrators, and all involved in public education was to convince students of this fact and thus enhance the value of schooling. All of us certainly have our ups and downs, but the value of education, in general, remains constant. My father told me this. My mother told me this, and most of us tell our children the same.

Status attainment in the United States, as most sociologists would agree, is the process by which individuals attain positions in the system of social stratification. If one thinks of social stratification as referring to the rewards society has to offer and the resources individuals use to obtain such rewards, education is most often the key factor in determining one's status. The degree and type of education people attain, in general terms, determines their level of employment and income. Certainly, everyone knows of exceptions. High school dropouts who become millionaires and Ph.D's who are taxi drivers. Education as a whole, and especially in the United States, is thought to be the great leveler. While this fact does not diminish the intrinsic value of learning for its own sake, from a socioeconomic point of view, education as measured by degrees and credentials is thought by most to be the primary tool of social mobility.

"Most U.S. public schools," as McDonald notes, "are, in effect, winnowing organizations where the worth of individuals is defined by very narrow criteria: one's grade point average, one's dutifulness in completing assignments, and one's capacity for speaking and thinking like the majority or elite group. For the majority of Americans, this process has been well accepted and functional."

The winnowing process in Westwood is so fine-tuned that student grade point averages (G.P.A.'s) are calculated down to the fourth decimal place to determine class rank, and I am sure that the standards are similarly refined in most school districts around the country. The vast majority of students with clear college bound expectations in Westwood know the game, how it is played, and where they stand. Parents who perceive their children as "college bound" also understand the process and reinforce it. Westwood teachers also have similar expectations. In the school district, it is not uncommon to hear teachers stating that they will be teaching the "Advanced Placement (A.P.)" group this semester, a "good" group, or on the other end of the scale, an "at-risk" population of students.

McDonald, in taking a different approach, says that all schools and teachers should believe in the same capacity of all their students, "to grow in knowledge, understanding, and social responsibility." He states, "Most schools do not believe this now." They are constrained from doing so by contrary psychological ideas that insist loudly or quietly that students' capacity is always limited and that schools can determine the limits in advance." I must confess I have often fallen into this trap and continue to struggle with the idea that all students can achieve at similarly high levels. I am also sometimes a victim of embracing a stratification-oriented approach to schooling.

My training in sociology has predisposed me to believe that perhaps more than any other in history, ours is an "open" society. Educational attainment is only weakly based upon parental status and predetermined conditions. I can personally relate to this statement since my mother did not graduate from high school and my father did not graduate from college.

This is not to say that I do not believe that some background variables have important influences especially when the issue of income is considered in the context of the relationships between education and occupational status and mobility. Frank Levy in *The New Dollars and Dreams - American Incomes and Economic Change* (1998) provides us with valuable insight especially with regard to the influence of race.

It is undeniable, as Levy notes, that great progress has been made during the last fifty years in terms of the relationship of one's race to occupational mobility. In 1949, less than two percent of employed black men were classified as managers or administrators; nearly six percent are today. In 1949, more than twenty percent of black men worked in agriculture, mostly as farm laborers; less than three percent have such jobs today. The picture is much cloudier, however, he says, when the frame of reference shifts from the last fifty years to the last twenty years. Since the mid-1970's, slow wage growth, the fall in the demand for less skilled men, crime, and the end of affirmative action have combined to slow substantially the progress of black males. Some similar trends can be identified for other racial groups but economic changes have hit black males particularly hard.

According to Levy in 1996, a reasonably good year economically with a national unemployment rate of 5.6 percent, 22 percent of working-age black males reported no earned income. Two-thirds of these men reported they were high school dropouts. While he notes that these data are probably exaggerated by unreported income, they remain startling. Many young black men felt, and continue to feel, alienated from school.

The causes of the problem relate to the restructuring and economic dislocation many central cities experienced during the mid-1970's, which the whole nation would experience after 1979--an accelerated loss of manufacturing jobs and losses in municipal employment, both of which reduced demand for semiskilled and unskilled workers. City employment was growing only in services that largely favored the better educated.

Reviewing the differences in the mobility of black and white men, Levy emphasizes that these issues also relate to quality and not just quantity of education. Consequentially, schools must be more sensitive to the needs and learning styles of young black men.

Jencks and Phillips (1998) attempt to address this problem by emphasizing that successful new interpretations of test scores and achievement gaps related to race will have to differ from prior research in several ways. "First, instead of emphasizing the kinds of racial and social background differences that economists and sociologists have traditionally studied (parents' economic resources, parents' position in the occupational hierarchy, parents' exposure to formal education, and parents' living arrangements), successful theories will take more account of the factors that psychologists have traditionally emphasized (the way family members interact with one another and with the outside world, for example.) And second, instead of looking mainly for resource differences between schools, successful theories will probably have to look more carefully at the way different groups of students respond to the same classroom experiences, such as being in a smaller classroom, having a more competent teacher, having a teacher of their own race, or having a teacher with high expectations for those who perform below the norm for their age group."

Jencks and Phillips, in addition, also argue that those who want to improve academic achievement should stop emphasizing factors such as the relationship between heredity and environment and stress the importance of a conservative and sometimes forgotten virtue, namely hard work. Americans currently seem all too ready to attribute academic failure to outside factors and/or low ability rather than to inadequate effort.

Jencks and Phillips, in supporting this argument, point to the work of Stevenson and Stigler (1998) who asked American, Japanese, and Taiwanese parents and teachers why some children did better than others in school. Interestingly, the Americans were more likely to emphasize ability, while the Japanese and Taiwanese were more likely to emphasize effort. These authors conclude, "This difference does not seem to reflect a difference in fundamental beliefs about causation. Children all over the world recognize that both ability and effort affect achievement, and the same is probably true for their parents as well. But attributing failure to inadequate effort implies that if you work harder, you will learn more. Attributing it to ability serves as an excuse for doing nothing."

Misinformation, despite the admonitions of these authors, however, continues to fuel the debate on student achievement and educational attainment. When the debate focuses on test scores, often the tendency is to blame institutions, the "system" or "social issues." Every teacher, administrator, and most parents are too familiar with the discourse.

Part of the problem is that the media often focuses public attention almost solely on the negatives associated with schools. As highlighted in a recent article entitled "Common Measures, Indicators of School Success -- Half-full, Half-empty" (*The American School Board (ASB) Journal*, December 1998), people around the country are more often than ever asking the question, "Are today's students getting a better or worse education than their parents?" Few ever ask the question, "Are students today working as hard in school as their counterparts of previous generations?"

According to the thirtieth annual Phi Delta Kappa/Gallup Poll of the Public's Attitudes toward Public Schools (1998), the answers to the first question are, as one would expect, mixed. Among the general population, 48 percent of those surveyed say education today is worse, 41 percent say it is better, eight percent say there is no difference, and three percent are not sure. The small number of those respondents who are not sure indicates the volatility of the question. Interestingly, parents of children in public schools are a bit happier than the general population, with 49 percent saying education is better and 43 percent saying it is worse; six percent see no difference, and two percent are undecided.

According to the Phi Delta Kappa/Gallup Poll, the results are similar to those in 1979 when the poll was initiated. A cause for alarm, however, is the fact that the 48 percent of the general population who believe that public education is getting worse is six percentage points higher than the 42 percent of the population who responded similarly in 1979. Unfortunately, the Phi Delta Kappa/Gallup Poll fails to distinguish what people mean by "better" or "worse." Nevertheless, the data continues to be published and take on meaning.

What should the new or prospective superintendent or central office administrator make of all this data? I would argue that he or she must be familiar with and focus on the different characteristics of the tested population and what parents perceive to be the most important issues.

In reviewing the Phi Delta Kappa/Gallup Poll (1998) discussed earlier, an additional important finding is the public's desire for smaller, more personal and user friendly schools. These data show that many parents continue to find schools unfriendly and unreceptive.

By way of contrast, in a recent National School Board Association survey, "Reaching for Excellence: What Local School Districts Are Doing To Raise Student Achievement (1998)," superintendents across the country identify the biggest roadblock to student achievement as lack of parent involvement. Some 68 percent of the superintendents surveyed say this is a moderate or serious problem in their districts. According to the superintendents, a close second is teachers' resistance to change, cited by 67 percent as a moderate or serious roadblock to student achievement.

Differing perceptions among parents, teachers, and students concerning their responsibility for academic achievement proved to be a challenge in Westwood and threatened the mutual trust I had worked to establish with the school committee. These factors collided as I was faced with a crucial decision experienced by almost every superintendent--how to interpret and, if necessary, enforce, school district policy as to what constitutes significant achievement and which students will graduate from high school in a given year.

Most superintendents view the months of May and June as both gratifying and joyfully anticipatory as they prepare for the graduation of yet another class of young people ready to meet the challenges of college or the world of work. These months, however, are also the most trying as superintendents face the appeals of parents whose children have not fulfilled graduation requirements.

In speaking to my colleagues throughout Rhode Island, I have learned that enforcing graduation requirements is, in a sense, a rite of passage for new superintendents. The new superintendent must hold the line, make no exceptions. Only students who have completed graduation requirements may walk across the stage and receive their diplomas. Despite parental requests to have students attend graduation and receive blank diplomas, every superintendent I have spoken with has indicated that no exceptions should be made. The principal of the high school certifies those students who have completed graduation requirements, and the superintendent affirms that ruling.

It is always a heart-wrenching encounter when parents cite any variety of family hardships--financial, social, emotional--as to why their children could not complete graduation requirements on time. Illness often comes into play or even, sometimes, criminal activity on the part of students. Principals and superintendents, however, must always hold the line and ensure that students have met school and district requirements to receive a diploma.

In spite of national achievement and related test score data, however, schools, principals, and superintendents must not ignore individual student needs. The case of Student Doe in Westwood conveys the complexities and emotions that I faced in confronting the dilemma of differentiating between individual and collective (school) responsibility for student achievement.

The Case of Student Doe

Normally, I would not provide specific details of a student's achievement in a forum such as this, but I only do so because the parent requested that this issue be aired in a public hearing. All of what I describe below was included in that hearing.

A week before Westwood High School's scheduled graduation on June 14, 1997, I was confronted with the demands of an extremely angry parent who complained that his son would not be graduating for lack of a required credit in United States History, a course he had failed that year due to lack of attendance. In addition to failing United States History in the twelfth grade, the student in question had also failed United States History in the tenth grade.

Although much of the anger of Student Doe's father focused on his son's failure to graduate, his wrath was also directed at the high school and administrative staff's late notification of this situation to the family. Such problems, as most administrators would agree, are common to many high schools across the country since final grades are tabulated on a tight timeline before graduation decisions are made.

As I researched the Student Doe situation, I also became aware of additional complexities related to the fact that the student in question was in an alternative school placement (Project SCOPE.) This program allowed him to receive credit for work experience. His placement complicated the problems I faced in evaluating the situation since the student worked late evening hours and then was scheduled into an early first period (7:35 A.M.) United States History class from which he was frequently absent (48 times) in the academic year in question--not the best scheduling/attendance situation.

The parent's questions regarding his son's pending failure to graduate were directed at all levels of the Westwood School Department's staff and administration and are summarized below. In many ways, they represent a new superintendent's nightmare.

Student Doe's Parents' Questions to Director, Project Scope:

1.   Was there a separate attendance policy in effect for the Project Scope Program? Who changed the attendance requirements whereby our son had to attend school early in the morning during his work week for one daily class when other students in the same program were not required to be in school in the morning?

2.   Our son logged over 2300 hours this past year maintaining a job as a condition of the Project Scope Program. He worked an average of 45 hours per week, sometimes more. What was the purpose of this requirement if it played no part in his final grades?

3.   Why was our son put into this program even though he clearly did not meet the requirements? To be eligible, academic requirements need to be met before the start of the senior year. This was not the case with our son since he needed to satisfy credits in English, Math, and United States History to graduate.

4.   On a couple of occasions, you called our home

and asked to speak to our son. Since I was the one who answered the phone, why did you neglect to inform me that there was a problem with his attendance?

5.   Why didn't you make a suggestion that our son be put into a class that met later in the morning? Why didn't you take steps, as the Director of this program, to remove him from it when you knew of his poor morning attendance and grades?

Student Doe's Parents' Questions to West Warwick's Director of Student Services:

1.   As Director of Student Services, at what point were you informed of our son's situation?

2.   If it were your job to oversee the operation of the Guidance Department, then you and those under your supervision failed miserably! The "buck" has been passed from person to person, and no one did anything to try and resolve the problem! Does everyone in that school walk around with blinders on? Wasn't there one person able to recognize the fact that there was a problem, or was it simply that no one cared? We get the impression that, unless you're an athlete or headed for college, no one is willing to help in any way.

3.   We find it hard to believe that your department did not know until June 9th that our son would not be graduating with his class. When are final grades turned in? When were programs, diplomas and caps and gowns ordered? To add

insult to injury, the fact that our son would not graduate didn't come from any school official; he had to tell us himself.

Student Doe's Parents' Questions to Westwood High School's United States History Teacher:

1. Why was our son denied the opportunity to make up two tests? Why did he have to sit out in the hall to take his final exam?

2. Why did you give our son false hope? He believed that making up whatever work you gave him, doing extra work, and earning a passing grade on the final exam would be enough to graduate.

3. When our son continued to miss class after being warned, why didn't you notify us yourself? It's not unusual for a teacher to notify parents if a problem exists. Why didn't you recommend that he be transferred to a later class?

4. His final grade was a 62, three points short of a passing grade of 65. Although our son missed classes, he made an effort. He made up whatever you allowed him to do. You were aware that he was missing class because of his work schedule, not because he was hanging out on street corners with his friends. You stated in our meeting that our son was not a problem in class. He wasn't disrespectful or a discipline problem. Given these circumstances, wasn't the effort our son made worth three points?

5.   You denied telling our son you were going to make an "example" of him. You stated in my presence that you wouldn't allow yourself to be labeled as a "pushover or easy teacher." You didn't want incoming students to believe they could be absent excessively and still be able to graduate. If this is not making an "example" of our son, then what is? Our son was the perfect "example" since he was the only senior in your class. It is quite obvious that protecting your image was more important than our son's graduation.

As the reader would expect, similar questions were addressed to me, the principal of Westwood High School, and the Westwood School Committee. The parents' comments to the school committee, at the open meeting to hear Student Doe's complaint, summarize their frustration. "This situation could have been avoided. We pleaded with everyone to find a way to reverse the decision. Everyone we spoke to insisted it was impossible. We don't believe that was true. We've heard of cases where exceptions were made and find it hard to believe the fact that who they were, and what they were involved in, had nothing to do with it."

The issues Student Doe's complaint presented to me as a new superintendent were numerous. At first glance, it would seem that I had a clear-cut choice to make: defend academics. Certainly, no student who failed United States History with 48 absences should graduate, I thought. Many other complexities, however, entered the picture. In part, the chairperson of the Westwood School Committee shared the parents' frustration with a bureaucratic high school, and, I must admit, in part, the less than comprehensive student monitoring program at the high school. Ultimately, I backed the history teacher's and principal's decision and did not allow Student Doe to graduate in June 1997.

The School Committee Chair, as a result of my approach to these issues, refused to acknowledge my presence at the June graduation. I began to think strongly about the viability of my tenure as superintendent in Westwood. I also contemplated applying for other positions and leaving the district. Cooler heads finally prevailed, and all learned from the experience. As the school committee chair and I mended fences, we agreed that the problems brought into focus by Student Doe's case were representative of those that would be encountered by many high schools across the United States -- a lack of a comprehensive monitoring process for at-risk students, sporadic communication with parents, and, at times, perpetuation of an impersonal environment.

In many ways, the case of Student Doe exemplifies the issue of individual versus collective responsibility for student achievement. I must say that I believe a parent should know if his/her son/daughter has missed 48 classes, failed to deliver progress reports, and failed United States History in the tenth grade and not made it up before graduation. These, however, are only my personal beliefs. As a Superintendent of Schools, I realize more must be done to personalize the educational environment. As I reviewed Westwood High School's handling of Student Doe's situation, I distilled the parents' complaints into four areas of inquiry. These questions and my responses are detailed as follows:

Q1.   **Did the teacher in question act appropriately in failing Student Doe in the course (U.S. History) that was required to graduate?**

Response: The teacher in question clearly indicated to the student what was expected of him in her class to receive credit.   The teacher maintained a comprehensive performance assessment plan that the student was aware of, which included homework and class participation. The teacher maintained an excellent record of student grades and attendance and completed required student progress reports.   In May 1997, her Progress Report on Student Doe indicated that he was excessively absent and that his homework and test results were incomplete. The teacher also communicated to the student's guidance counselor that the student's attendance was poor and should "be looked into." The teacher set and maintained reasonable and attainable standards for her class.

Q2.   **What role did Westwood High School administration/guidance play in decisions regarding Student Doe's academic progress and subsequent failure to graduate on June 14, 1997?**

Response: This area was the most complicated aspect of the investigation and revealed the following:

A.   The Westwood High School Principal, Director of Student Services, and Guidance Counselor were all aware of Student Doe's situation and intervened in a number of ways including: 1. sending an April 1997, letter to Student Doe's parents expressing concerns (which the parents state they did not receive), 2. meeting with Student Doe to express concern and issue warnings, 3. issuing a May, 1997, Progress Report to Student Doe (which the parents state they didn't review until after June 9, 1997), 4. calling the student's home and leaving messages regarding poor attendance.

B. While there is verbal confirmation and corroboration on the part of Westwood High School regarding issuance of warnings to both Student Doe and his parents concerning his academic situation, it must also be stated that no written record (such as U.S. Post Office return receipt/requested slip) exists to document these interventions with the exception of the May, 1997, Progress Report indicating the student's excessive absences and incomplete academic work.

C. Issues continue to exist as to whether the student's academic placement (Project Scope) as an alternative part-time work and school schedule was the most appropriate placement for him. According to the statements of the student's guidance counselor, this was, in fact, the best alternative for an at-risk student. Questions, however, remain as to whether an alternative afternoon United States History course schedule might have yielded different outcomes than a 7:40 A.M. start time.

Given all the circumstances, it was my finding that the administration generally performed appropriately in response to student Doe's predicament. The issue, however, remains as to whether new policies or practices should be formalized to document communications with parents.

Q3.   **What respective responsibility did Student Doe and his parents have in his failure to graduate?**

Response: In addition to the Westwood High School administration, it is clear that both parents and Student Doe share responsibility for the issue at hand. A summary of the facts follows.

• Student Doe was informed of academic and attendance concerns by his U.S. History teacher and guidance counselor and principal on a number of occasions.

• Student Doe did not provide his parents with a copy of his May 1997 Progress Report until June 1997.

• Student Doe's parents did contact the guidance counselor in April 1997, and were told that the student "should graduate" if he continued to perform to standards.

- It would seem that the parents should have been aware of Student Doe's excessive absences and taken action to remediate the situation.

A clear question remains as to what role the parents might have played in holding Student Doe accountable for his attendance.

Finally, in summary, it is clear that Student Doe's failure to graduate from Westwood High School on June 14, 1997, was devastating to the parents and student and revealed an unusual set of circumstances, especially given that the student had attained "Honors" status for the third quarter of the 1996-97 school year.

It is equally clear, however, that the administration was correct in not approving the student for graduation in that he had not completed a required United States History course, which he had also failed in the tenth grade and could have made up in that year's summer school session.

While it is apparent that the Westwood High School staff intervened on a number of occasions to help ensure Student Doe's successful completion of graduation requirements, it should also be noted that the parents' complaint as to early and up-to-date notification of their son's status calls into question certain policies and practices of Westwood High School and the Westwood School Department.

As a result of Student Doe's complaint, a number of new procedures were initiated at Westwood High School that became an early warning system for students at risk of not graduating with their class.

As is the case with most public high schools, Westwood High School has a fairly large number of students at risk of not graduating each year for a variety of reasons. These reasons include the student not obtaining enough credits, possible failure in required courses -- English, mathematics, science or history -- or failure to meet the school's attendance requirements. In addition, at-risk students, like Student Doe, may have failed to comply with alternative program requirements previously agreed to by the student, parents, and school. Consequently, the Westwood administrative staff and I developed a number of provisions intended to improve both school/student and school/parent communication. In December of each year, the high school principal compiles a list of seniors who run the risk of not graduating and communicates this possibility to parents through certified mail. The principal clearly states what steps must be taken to rectify the problems.

Past policy relied on the November report card to convey this message to students and parents. A personalized approach seems more effective. As part of the new communication process, parents are also requested to call the high school to discuss their son or daughter's situation. Additionally, the December communication is followed by a certified letter in March informing parents of their child's progress in meeting previous deficiencies and of any new ones that may have emerged. Furthermore, the principal meets with at-risk seniors (46 in 1998) in a March assembly and sets up individual counseling sessions with each student. Finally, in May, the principal and guidance department provide an additional warning to both parents and students. A key point of this intervention also involves providing strong tutorial support to those students at risk of not graduating. In March of 1997, students were offered the option of attending "Saturday School," which essentially is the equivalent of a traditional summer school program offering comprehensive instruction in three-hour blocks to address academic deficiencies.

Most faculty members at Westwood High School agree that the comprehensive intervention program for at-risk seniors has been an overall success. The resulting benefits include: (1) a reduction in tension and parent complaints prior to June graduation, (2) an increase in the graduation rate, (3) a three-year decrease in the dropout rate from 29.6% to 21.6% partially due to this program.

These efforts, however, have not been without detractors. A small, though vociferous, number of teachers have complained to the superintendent that standards have fallen with the introduction of "Saturday School." In effect, their argument has been that if students cannot meet requirements during the traditional school year, they should not be able to graduate with their designated class. The appropriate way for these students to graduate, these teachers have argued, should be through summer school attendance thereby not diminishing the recognition bestowed upon their classmates who complete their requirements during the regular year. Partially, I am in agreement with the reservations of these teachers; however, my thinking has evolved and, and as I stated earlier, I recognize that a more personal approach is needed to meet individual student needs.

As I researched the reasons why many at-risk seniors were in danger of not graduating, it became clear that social and family problems were contributing factors; however, many students who thrive in traditional programs have managed to overcome these obstacles.

Chapter 8

Supervision of Principals and Staff

Two conflicting thoughts come to mind when I reflect upon a superintendent's responsibility to oversee the performance of principals. I am reminded of the advice of two people I admire for their devotion to improving public education. Timothy Sullivan, a great friend who served as Wellton's Superintendent of Schools for ten years through the 1980's, later became Superintendent of Schools in Bloomington, Minnesota, and now serves as Superintendent in Danbury, Connecticut, once advised me, "Be good to and support your principals -- they will be around much longer than most school committee members." The second piece of advice comes from Tom Silva, former Chairperson of the Westwood School Committee. "Michael--watch your administrators (principals)--they are the ones who will get you into trouble." Both Tim and Tom were right, Tim perhaps a bit more than Tom. During my tenure in Westwood, supervision and support of principals have presented challenges to me, but the latter have not outweighed the collegial support principals have provided. As everyone associated with public education knows, the role of a principal is one of the most demanding imaginable. The following satirical job description suggests the extent of their responsibilities:

A Principal's Job Description

This thing I submit for consideration
A principal MUST HAVE a great education
(Ain't no foolin' he's gotta have lots of schoolin')
He must make many preparations
To fulfill the diverse qualifications.
So here's a description of his job
Oh, the things he must do -- they're a mob!

He Must:
1. Count the money and answer the phone.
2. Talk to ten people at once -- all alone.
3. Make arrangements for a bus that's broken down.
4. Pick up checks all the way downtown.
5. Find the set screw to fix a projector.
6. Get some cars moved for the garbage collector.
7. Arbitrate children's quarrels and fights.
8. Talk to parents on PTA nights.

9.   Decide just when a skirt is too short.
10.   Appear, because of a burglary, in court.
11.   Dictate a form for permission slips.
12.   Decide how much to charge on field trips.
13.   Check over the menu for next week's lunch.
14.   Take care of the "sent to the office" bunch.
15.   Fill out a blankety-blank federal form.
16.   Check the furnace -- the building's not warm.
17.   Be on time to the principal's meeting.
18.   Meet a new parent with a suitable greeting.
19.   Fix the mower -- the grass is knee-high.
20.   Try to deduce which kid told a lie.
21.   Rush up the hall -- water is pouring from a tank.
22.   Rush down the hall and get to the bank.

Then the bell rings, teachers leave one by one.
Alone at last -- to get his work done!

Presented in fun by:
FREEDOM INDUSTRIES
The Spirit & Pride Builders
for America's Schools
Murfreesboro, TN 37130
615-896-3800

The responsibilities of a principal run the gamut from the mundane to the sublime. The position requires great energy, dedication, intelligence, leadership qualities, and a great sense of humor.

One of the important management initiatives taken in Westwood, as previously mentioned, involved reconfiguring the deployment of principals in the district and the elimination of elementary assistant principals. Long-term test results and dropout data will be the true measures of my actions. Many principals, while recognizing the value of my policy decisions, have expressed concerns that the elimination of elementary assistant positions has made their work more difficult in terms of responding to parental requests for information and services, especially in the area of discipline. I accept the principals' criticisms and have worked to provide additional support on a variety of fronts including the creation of disciplinary aide positions, the establishment of a district-wide attendance committee to deal with truancy issues, and a district-wide technology committee. A great deal, however, still needs to be done especially in the area of student discipline and improved outreach and accountability to parents.

In addition to these issues, three of the elementary schools and the middle and high schools have experienced changes in leadership. As new administrators came into the district, the assistant superintendent and I have provided them with a solid orientation. Faculty meetings with new administrators were held, "meet the principal" meetings were convened with parents, each principal received a comprehensive evaluation at six-month and one-year intervals. As part of the evaluation process, goals for each administrator were agreed upon and ongoing site observations were conducted.

Certainly more could have been done. Although goal setting and instructional objectives were emphasized, less time was spent on the nitty-gritty and oftentimes most troublesome aspect of school administration: student, parent, and faculty complaints. As future administrators enter the district, I plan to spend much more time on role playing and case study types of professional development activities. On a minute-by-minute basis, principals deal successfully with these issues; however, parent, faculty, and student complaints take on a different aspect when they reach the superintendent's office or the school committee. Often the response of superintendents involves post facto or hindsight advice or analysis. One of the challenges involved in supervising a new administrator, as Stephen B. Fisher emphasizes (Jentz, 1982), is to balance the need for freedom and independence with the need for support and guidance of the individual being supervised.

Fisher recounts his initial "Sink or Swim: Laid Back/On His Back" approach to supervising a new assistant principal. The hiring process for the person in question, he recalls, was a good one. It involved faculty members from various departments who asked questions that assessed the candidate's problem solving ability and his/her likely performance in simulated stress situations during initial interviews. The candidate emerged from this process seemingly confident and was looking forward to his first administrative position. Fisher recalls that he thought the candidate was a good choice and looked forward to working with him. He lasted only one painful year. What went wrong?

Fisher remembers, "Without knowing it, I threw the new administrator to the wolves. I thought I had hired a competent and capable individual, and so assumed that it was my responsibility to maximize that person's freedom by leaving him alone to develop his style and solve problems with students, parents, and staff." As Fisher recalls, he provided little supervision to the new administrator, and no mentoring program was in place. The new man on the scene was left to sink or swim on his own.

Fisher, like most administrators, welcomed his new assistant with the assurance, "I am here, if you need me." What he should have made clear, however, was, "If you can't hack it, come see me." As Fisher notes, he had, in effect, established a scenario that asking for advice was an admission of failure. A common mistake.

Fisher further admits that he exacerbated the situation by solving staff, school, and discipline problems that the new assistant should have solved himself. By injecting himself into the situation, Fisher rescued him from difficulties, which seemed the responsible thing to do. Such intervention, however, robbed the new administrator of the opportunity to develop the independence and skill necessary to succeed.

Fisher concludes, "This pattern of supervision contributed to the failure of the new administrator by keeping him 'on a string,' and increasingly 'unsure' of himself." He kept getting mixed messages: "Go ahead. Stop! Go ahead. Stop!" Ultimately, the new administrator felt undermined, abandoned, and used."

This state of affairs is also referred to by Reeves (1998) who states, "The most constant complaint I have heard from school administrators around the country is that they are being held accountable for things over which they have no control." One has a tendency to confuse visibility with effective performance, Reeves (1998) observes, and rewards principals who are better at self-promotion than instructional leadership. An added stumbling block for administrators is to place too much emphasis on those who subscribe to the popular concept of seeking outside input in decision making. This approach, while intended to build collegiality, has its limits, particularly if the standard for the final decision is not what is best for student achievement but what is deemed most popular.

"Almost no one doubts that accountability by school leaders is imperative," Reeves concludes. "Certainly the goal of improved student achievement is best achieved not by intimidation and threats, but by a system that focuses on academic achievement while providing specific and meaningful feedback to students, teachers, and leaders."

Given the duties and responsibilities of principals, their needs for supervision and support by superintendents are almost endless and often frustrating. One of the concerns I have as a superintendent is the time constraint under which I must often operate. I am called upon sometimes to help manage a crisis or solve a problem, but do not have an opportunity to see the situation through to completion because of other commitments. I attempt to do what is required and expected and must leave others to complete the final details. To this end, I am sometimes envious when I hear a principal use the words, "my school" or "my students." The superintendent's role is by definition detached, reserved, and fragmented. The simple fact is that if one stays in a school until all its problems are solved, other problems are left unsolved in other schools.

On a day-to-day basis, most schools and principals operate efficiently and effectively on an internal basis managing problems related to student discipline, faculty supervision, and parent complaints. When issues come to the superintendent's attention, they usually involve gray areas requiring further interpretation, legal advice, or the need for the superintendent to assess school committee political perceptions related to the problem at hand. My office recently initiated a modest research project cross-referencing all telephone calls received over a two-month period regarding administrative practices in the district. Calls were categorized by types of issues and the particular school or central office function they addressed. They were then cataloged as to whether they were directed to functions of the central office or individual schools, and those directed to the central office were sorted into major categories.

These findings unexpectedly indicated that the largest number of calls fell into the legal category, and as one might expect, most of the other calls were routine. Selected types of calls in the routine category included: requests for employment applications, requests for time and date of school activities, school busing complaints, questions regarding school district policies, budget questions, and sales calls. New to the superintendent's role, the latter type of call involving solicitation was one that I had not anticipated and often found to be annoying.

Interestingly, the smallest number of calls to the superintendent's office centered on instructional practices. Given the range of issues discussed in Chapter 7 regarding student achievement, it is ironic that this was the least discussed topic. As would be expected, routine administration calls were most frequent.

Finally in reviewing the overall data, until one sits in the superintendent's chair, it is difficult to imagine the time one spends on legal issues. Part of the problem is that so much time is spent by attorneys going to and fro attempting to negotiate agreements and out-of-court settlements, activities that require superintendent and school committee input. For new superintendents, it is easy to underestimate the time they must spend behind the scenes explaining legal issues to committee members while attempting to develop consensus prior to open public meetings.

Presently, there are many ongoing lawsuits in Westwood, some of which include: litigation related to the termination of the prior superintendent, indictment of a principal on child sexual abuse charges, a federal discrimination suit filed by a student and his parents. These time-consuming suits impinge upon a superintendent's schedule and hinder his ability to focus on principals' professional development.

Discipline and student behavior issues, as one might expect, were difficult to address at the school level and presented a variety of problems for a new superintendent. Following are five of the most difficult situations I've had to face; prospective superintendents may benefit from my experience.

Scenario 1
Punishing the Group for the "Sins" of The Individual

During my experience in Westwood and Wellton, a common complaint I received regarding principals was their tendency to sometimes punish large groups of students when only segments of the group had violated school rules. Most of these cases involved elementary school recess and lunchtime infractions.

Many of us can recall a principal admonishing a group of children, "If you're not quiet right now, you're all going to stay after school." While I can appreciate the principal's desire for order, I have often received complaints from parents whose children went home justifiably stating that they were quiet but were punished because their fellow students did not behave. I can think of few occasions where punishment of a group is justified because of the transgressions of a limited number of students. As I advise principals, it is much better to single out an individual or small groups of offenders and discipline them rather than the large group.

Scenario 2
The Book Bag Incident

Although this scenario may be difficult to believe, one of the most unusual intervention situations I experienced with a principal in Westwood involved what has come to be referred to as the famous "book bag" incident. This incident provides insight into a bizarre aspect of a superintendent's day.

A principal forwarded the following message to my office during the Winter of 1997, "One of my fifth grade students just ran into the school to tell me that there was a big book bag moving at the bus stop around the corner. I went out to investigate, and sure enough, there was a moving book bag. As I looked inside, a crying, perspiring, and urine soaked little boy about four or five years old jumped out. When I asked him what happened, he said his older brother had stuffed him in the bag and dragged him to the bus stop. The little boy then ran away before I could catch him. I returned to school and questioned other children who were at the bus stop. At that point, I was able to learn the identity of the child and went to his house to see if he was all right. His mother said he was fine and I returned to school."

The incident was reviewed to determine if anything should have been handled differently. For the most part, the principal and I agreed that the situation was handled well. It occurred to me, however, to ask the principal if he had actually seen the little boy to determine his condition when he visited the home. The principal replied that he had not. My reaction was to call the police, return to the home, and assess the boy's condition to ensure that he had not been injured or abused.

Upon arriving at the home, we were allowed to see the boy and learned that he had injured his head. Unknown to the principal on his prior visit was the fact that when the little boy had been placed in the bag by his nine-year old brother, he had been dragged down a flight of stairs, and he had bumped his head a number of times. The mother agreed that the younger boy needed emergency medical help, and an ambulance was called. The little boy though bruised was released later that day in his mother's custody.

An aspect of this case, which came to light as the older boy was interviewed, was that he had gotten the idea to place his brother in the book bag from a book entitled *Show and Tell* by Munsch and Martchenko, which he had borrowed from his school's library.

This book tells the story of a boy named Benjamin who wanted to take something really neat to school for show-and-tell and decided to take his new baby sister. The author states, "So he went upstairs, picked her up while she was sleeping, put her into his knapsack and walked off to school." Munsch and Martchenko go on to re-count, "But when he sat down, his baby sister finally woke up. She was not happy inside the knapsack and started to cry. The teacher looked at him and said, 'Benjamin, stop making that noise.' Ben said, 'That's not me. It's my baby sister. She's in my knapsack. I brought her for show-and-tell.' 'Yikes!' said the teacher', You can't keep a baby in a knapsack.' She grabbed Ben's knapsack and opened it up. The baby looked at the teacher and said, 'WAAA, WAAA, WAAA, WAAA, WAAA!!' " One just never knows the full impact of curriculum and library resources.

While this case was certainly unusual, there have been many others that have tested the detective skills of Westwood's principals and my abilities to assist them. Another of these cases included the flame-thrower makers.

Scenario 3
The Flame-thrower Makers

In the Fall of 1998, I received a call from a parent stating that her son's face had been burned and that she would not allow him to attend Westwood's middle school ever again. While speaking to the middle school principal, I learned that on the afternoon in question, the principal received a call from the mother who said that her son had been on or near middle school property when other boys burned his face. The principal was wise to advise the mother to call the police. He, however, in the middle of a busy day, failed to notify my office of the police call, which is a violation of a district policy, which states "The superintendent's office must be notified within one hour when police or fire personnel are called to school property." It was a simple oversight on his part. My office having no knowledge of the call had a significant impact, however, in that the school committee chair had already been informed of the incident and was upset that I hadn't known of it.

I learned what had actually happened as a result of the police investigation. During the afternoon in question, three middle school students stole a can of aerosol gum remover from the custodian's closet, fitted it with a large nozzle, walked to the sidewalk adjacent to the school, and activated it while holding a cigarette lighter flame to the spray, creating a twelve to sixteen inch flame. The mother who called me stated that her son happened to be walking by at the time and was singed but not seriously burned by the flame. Since the boys responsible for the incident had not intentionally sought to harm the victim, they were not charged with assault but were disciplined through the school's "zero tolerance" policy. Another example which illustrates the problems involving communication between principals' and superintendents' offices is the "sucker punch" incident.

Scenario 4
The "Sucker Punch" Incident

One day in late December as Christmas approached, I decided to visit each school to wish faculties a joyful holiday season. My standard routine was to advise the principal of my presence and then tour each school in his/her company. On one such occasion, as I turned the corner from the principal's office at an elementary school accompanied by the acting assistant principal, we encountered a very angry teacher with a group of students. As soon as I saw the teacher, I knew something was seriously wrong when I heard a loud and angry voice stating, "You punched me and now it's my turn." I couldn't believe what I was hearing and the acting assistant principal looked at me incredulously as if to ask, "What do I do?" I told him to confront the teacher immediately! At first he seemed unsure but followed my advice. As acting assistant principal, I thought it was his responsibility to take the lead because I did not want to appear to be usurping his authority, and I was concerned about his lack of confidence in what to do. Essentially, I thought the incident would provide him with a good learning experience. Had I not been there, he might have decided to confront the teacher at a later time. New principals, I believe, must be encouraged to handle health and safety issues wisely and promptly. The acting assistant principal in question learned from the incident and, I am certain, grew professionally.

Questioning the teacher while another teacher and I accompanied the students to class, he learned that the instant before we saw the teacher lash out, he had been heartily punched in the solar plexus by a hefty fifth-grader. The teacher's angry reaction was to tell the student that he was in for a taste of his own medicine.

The assistant principal and I had just witnessed the aftermath of this sneak punch. The teacher's reaction, however, to my way of thinking, was unjustified. Although I could empathize with his anger, I could not accept his manner of dealing with an incident which could have escalated into a much more serious situation.

Based on my interpretation of the events, I relieved the teacher of his duties for the remainder of the day with pay and directed him to report to my office that afternoon. During the meeting, the teacher expressed the opinion that I had overreacted by relieving him of his duties. My response was that although I understood his reaction, I still believed his behavior to be inappropriate. The rationale supporting my decision was and continues to be twofold. First and foremost, I believe that all teachers, administrators, and staff must work constantly to avoid escalating confrontations with students. In this case, I believe the teacher's actions definitely bordered on escalating the situation. Secondly, I also believe it is the superintendent's responsibility to act swiftly and decisively when dealing with actions not in the best interests of students. A better course of action on the teacher's part would have been to maintain his composure, inform the student of his inappropriate behavior, and notify the principal's office of a violation of the district's code and the fact that he had been assaulted.

Certainly, this was an incident that other administrators or superintendents might have reacted to differently; however, the manner in which they handle school conflicts depends primarily on their personal administrative styles.

Scenario 5
Time to Hold One's Tongue

In an increasingly media saturated society, situations where negative publicity is created by saying the wrong thing at the wrong time are all too common. Sometimes such comments are made from ignorance or result from a lack of appreciation for appropriate decorum.

Among the worst instances of someone saying the wrong thing at the wrong time is Los Angeles Dodgers' General Manager Al Companis's comments on the association between race and athletic performance. On the more humorous side, such "faux pas" have included those by former aide to President Clinton, George Stephanopolous, who, while appearing on the "Larry King Live Show", stated, "The President has kept all of the promises he intended to keep," and Mrs. Clinton's comment on the release of subpoenaed documents, "I'm not going to have some reporter pawing through our papers. We are the President!"

The worst situation of having the wrong thing said at the wrong time that I experienced as a Superintendent of Schools involved a Westwood teacher. In early December of 1997, I received a telephone call from the high school principal describing the following incident. That morning, a male high school student had been disruptive in home economics class and when confronted by the teacher, responded by throwing a soiled towel in her face. The teacher's impulsive reaction was, "Your mother should have had an abortion!" Within a day, the incident was covered by local and regional print, radio, and television media throughout New England.

Immediately following the incident, the high school principal and I caucused and implemented a discipline protocol whereby the boy was suspended from school, and the teacher received a written reprimand and complied with our request to provide the boy and his mother with a written apology for her remark. Our decision took into consideration the teacher's unblemished history of more than twenty years of service to the school district as well as the boy's prior history of discipline code violations. While we realized our decision might result in controversy, we thought it was a sound choice. That the student in question was from a racially mixed background and the teacher was white complicated the issue.

The incident became grist for Providence, Rhode Island, radio and television talk shows and for editorial writers throughout the state. The range of comments ran the gamut from the decision being appropriate, too harsh to the boy, too harsh to the teacher, too lenient for both. Some called for the teachers' dismissal; others called for the boy's suspension from school for the remainder of the year.

Making matters worse, the teacher, upon the advice of legal counsel, filed an assault complaint against the boy for throwing the towel, and the boy's mother filed a discrimination suit with the U.S. Department of Civil Rights. Although the media frenzy eventually calmed down, legal maneuvering continued for months until both parties agreed to allow the case to go to mediation provided by the Department of Civil Rights.

The mediator's excellent work resulted in an appropriate accommodation - a 504 plan for the boy. The trepidation caused by the incident among administration and faculty continues to linger. All parties concerned are now better aware of how stress can build and the need for improved ways of managing it. When discussing the incident with the teacher, she stated that she just didn't know what had happened and that she knew she had said something very wrong the moment the words left her mouth.

As superintendent, the situation was especially difficult because I was simultaneously attempting to support the teacher, student, and principal through this difficult time while attempting to manage the public relations storm that had been created. Certainly, there is no perfect formula for dealing with the media in such situations, but my advice includes attempt to stay calm, be forthright with responses, respect all the parties involved.

Another incident involving ill-timed and inappropriate statements by a Westwood employee occurred when a secretary was charged with contributing to a hostile work environment by one of her colleagues. Hostile work environment charges usually arise when one or more employees engage in sexually suggestive or insulting comments, displays of sexually suggestive material, or other offending behaviors that contribute to or create uncomfortable or untenable work environments for their colleagues. Such situations are especially difficult for supervisors to handle because other employees not directly involved often tend to take sides and support either the victim or victims or the alleged contributor or contributors to the hostile work environment. Cases of hostile work environment complaints that are sustained by the courts usually result from offenses that took place over a period of time contributing to the distress of victims and eventually compromise their ability to perform their duties.

The Westwood hostile work environment complaint followed a similar pattern. On more than one occasion, the offending party had made what could be considered sexually suggestive comments to her colleague. This pattern of comments came to a head when a male co-employee made an inappropriate comment which included a reference to a sexual act which prompted a comment by the offending party to suggest inappropriate and highly offensive sexual activity by the victim.

Following this last incident, the victim lodged a hostile work environment complaint with me and immediately retained an attorney. Based upon my investigation of the allegation made and the incidents described above, it was clear that a hostile work environment had existed.

While I had not received any prior complaint or notice by fellow employees of the offending party regarding her comments and actions, I nevertheless regret that I did not assume a stronger posture with regard to preventing such office behavior. As superintendent, I had ensured that the district had an up-to-date sexual harassment policy. I now believe that more could have been done in terms of prevention and educating employees on related topics.

A number of attorneys have told me that the mere existence of a sexual harassment policy is not sufficient to protect an employer from liability. As part of their regular dissemination of harassment policies, employers should also consider providing "consciousness raising" or awareness training sessions to all employees and train supervisors as to how complaints should be properly handled. *Bouton v. BMW of North America, Inc.,* 1994 U.S. App Lexis 20755 (3rd Cir., 65 Emp. Proc. Guide (CCH) 43,185; *Andrews v. Philadelphia*, 895 F.2d 1469 (3rd Cir. 1990) are legal precedents that provide useful related information on a topic that all superintendents and employees would like to avoid. Unfortunately, dealing with unprofessional conduct, sexual harassment, and related issues have comprised a major portion of my administrative experiences in Westwood.

Chapter 9

The Superintendent as Investigator and Prosecutor

Mary Jane Cooper (1998) writes that the unthinkable sometimes happens, and superintendents must face the task of investigating allegations that a principal or a teacher has had inappropriate sexual relations or contact with a student. Such situations quickly become nightmarish as one tries to separate fact from fiction. These cases often tear a school district apart when teachers, parents, and community members take sides in supporting the alleged victim or perpetrator. Usually, it is an untenable situation for the superintendent and an easy way to make enemies on either side of the issue. How the superintendent reacts is important.

Newspaper headlines such as the following reveal some of the problems I faced in Westwood: *Community Stunned By Arrest of Principal; Acclaimed Principal Put on Indefinite Leave; Indictment of Principal Casts Pall on School Committee Swearing-In Ceremony; Teacher Faces Hearing on Complaint of Harassment; Teacher Loses Final Two Days of Pay for Sexual Misconduct.*

My initiation into the process of investigating allegations of staff misconduct of this sort began when I was called to an emergency meeting with Westwood's Chief of Police. When summoned, I immediately sensed the tension in the room and the seriousness of his mood. Straight away, the Chief informed me that a teenage male, a former Westwood elementary and high school student, had filed a complaint of sexual assault against a popular and effective elementary principal whom I will refer to as Principal A.

A November 1998, local newspaper account exemplifies the town's reaction to the allegations. Westwood needed Principal A. the article began. "He grew up here. To Westwood residents, he was their teacher, their children's Little League coach, Sunday School instructor, youth programs leader and, eventually, elementary school principal."

At the time of the pending allegations, I immediately placed Principal A. on paid administrative leave while the people associated with his school carried knowledge of the ongoing investigation as an uneasy secret. Faculty at the school were shattered and in a state of disbelief. Many questioned my judgment in taking the allegations seriously. Others, more objectively, took an innocent until proven guilty stance, but recognized the need for a thorough investigation.

While I had had some prior training on how to deal with similar situations, I nevertheless took a refresher course on the subject with two school attorneys and representatives of the State Department of Education. The key elements of this training focused on four general themes:

Legal Protocols

The superintendent, in Rhode Island and most other states, is responsible for conducting investigations of alleged unprofessional and/or illegal conduct by staff, independent of police investigations. This means, in simple terms, that the superintendent may reach corroborating or differing conclusions than those reached by legal authorities regarding allegations. It is also advisable, in addition, for the superintendent to use outside legal counsel, preferably a firm different from the district's regular legal representation, which I did in the case of Principal A. Retaining independent legal counsel is almost a prerequisite and an expense that cannot be avoided for superintendents conducting independent investigations into allegations like those lodged against Principal A. Both the accuser and the accused have legal rights that must be protected, and the superintendent must work to ensure that the school committee follows all relevant policies, procedures, and laws as investigations proceed. Some of the most relevant aspects of Rhode Island law include teachers' rights to receive compensation while investigations proceed and their rights to full hearings before their school committee prior to deprivation of salary or benefits. In addition, the school committee in question must furnish the teacher with a complete statement of cause(s) when suspension of a property right is initiated and, of course, teachers have the right of appeal for any related action a school committee might take.

Staff Support/Transition

Staff, in most cases, are in a state of disbelief when allegations like those lodged against Principal A. surface. Related reactions certainly complicate the superintendent's role. In addition to making available professional counseling to teachers, parents, and students in Westwood, I also met with staff members and attempted, in general terms, to apprise them of my investigation. While these meetings were difficult, by and large, I found them to be productive. Part of the staff support plan included the recruitment of highly qualified veteran substitute administrators for Principal A. The professionalism of these individuals was invaluable during a difficult period.

School Committee/Superintendent Communications

The superintendent's role investigating professional or criminal misconduct is difficult; so too is the school committee's. Most difficult is the fact that even though the school committee should not participate in the superintendent's investigations, it is still under pressure to respond to the questions asked by parents, staff, and media. Since school committees might later have to sit in judgment regarding the superintendent's determinations, their maintaining an objective position is crucial.

Media Relations

Media attention to cases like that of Principal A. are intense and stressful for any superintendent. Attempting to balance the public's right to know with the need to maintain confidentiality rights of all parties is essential.

Those accused of misconduct and their supporters, in most cases, want to maintain a "lid" on related publicity while parents and the general community expect clear communication and proper updates. The superintendent, as usual, is in the middle.

Kathy Jacks, a Westwood mother who works at the Rhode Island Rape and Sexual Assault Center, summed up public sentiment in Westwood when she said, "People are reacting just as you'd expect when a person of esteem is the target of an investigation: there's a lot of disbelief, a lot of 'it can't be.' It always shocks people when an offender is someone they trust. But so often the accused in child molestation cases is the most trusted: the priest, the coach, the day care provider, a family member -- the trusted person, the nice one."

Jacks also recommends that parents talk to their children, not only about sexual assault, but also about how respected adults can get into trouble. "It really depends on how it is explained to them. Kids hear things, and they need to know people make mistakes. They need to know that even people we like can do things that aren't right."

In June of 1999, Principal A. pleaded guilty to one count of second-degree child molestation, encompassing the instances of fondling and oral sex that occurred over a three-year period until the victim turned fourteen. Resulting from an agreement with prosecutors, Principal A. was sentenced to twenty years in prison with all twenty of these years suspended in exchange for his agreeing to register legally as a child molester and agreeing to twenty years' probation.

Based on my investigation and his prior indictment for related charges, I had placed the principal on leave without pay on November 19, 1997. Little did I know that this suspension would leave him fifteen days shy of completing enough service to draw a lifetime annual $37,759.00 pension at the age of 49. Under the Rhode Island retirement system regulations, employees can collect their pensions before age sixty if they have credit for 28 years of service. As a result of his suspension, Principal A.'s pension clock stopped at 27 years and nine months requiring him to wait another eleven years to receive benefits. In addition, he will most likely lose his license to teach or serve as a public school administrator. Principal A.'s case, however, was only the first of three I dealt with in Westwood where staff members faced sexually related criminal complaints.

The Providence Journal (June 13, 1999) notes that my problems with sexually related complaints in Westwood over such a short time span are likely unparalleled in the state's history and most probably more numerous than those encountered in most school districts of similar size in the United States. Sexual misconduct cases, according to the Rhode Island Department of Education, are fairly rare with only about a dozen resulting in teacher certificate revocations during the 1990's.

The second case I encountered involved Teacher B. This allegation concerned a parent's complaint that a Westwood female science teacher had a sexual relationship with his son. Based on information from Westwood's Chief of Police, I learned that nearby Creighton police had investigated this complaint, but that charges had been dropped because at the time of the alleged incident the boy was sixteen years old, the age of consent in Rhode Island.

Complicating matters, Westwood police also identified a second student who alleged that he had had a sexual relationship with the teacher eight years earlier when he was fifteen years old. While this boy was not of the age of consent when the relationship allegedly occurred, I was later informed that in this case Rhode Island's three-year statute of limitations had expired. The outcomes of these police investigations clearly pointed to the need for a superintendent's parallel investigation. While no police charges were filed in either case, strong evidence of unprofessional conduct on the part of Teacher B. remained. My investigation, in effect, had to determine if a higher standard of professional conduct should apply than that defined by criminal codes.

The United States Department of Education (Crisci, 1999) offers important assistance to education administrators involved in such investigations. According to Department guidelines, information involved in a superintendent's investigation should include statements by witnesses; assessments of the relative credibility of student witnesses, evidence that the alleged perpetrator has engaged in inappropriate conduct with others; the alleged victim's reaction or behavior after the supposed inappropriate behavior (remembering, however, that a delayed reaction is possible); evidence of a complaint or other action the victim took to protest the conduct (also remembering that some victims will not complain out of fear); and evidence that the student may have written about the conduct in a diary or letter or told friends, parents, or others about it shortly after it occurred.

According to United States Department of Education Guidelines, a sexual relationship between an employee and an elementary student is never regarded as consensual. An employee may be terminated and prosecuted for a sexual relationship regardless of the student's age.

The U.S. Department of Education, in effect, begins by assuming that no student offers consent. In doing so, it reviews the nature of the conduct and the relationship of the employee to the student, including the degree of authority the employee has over the student, and examines whether the student was able to consent to the sexual conduct.

Several other factors should be considered including the degree to which the incident affected the student's education, grade, or participation in activities; physical injuries or stress; the type, frequency, or duration of the conduct; and the relationship between the individuals.

Cooper (1998) reinforces how these complexities should enter into the superintendent's investigation. She especially emphasizes how alleged victims may deny that relationships occurred even if they did. High school students in a number of cases may be willing in the beginning to participate in inappropriate relationships, might not want relationships to end, or might not want to get their teachers in trouble. These students recognize that if their relationships come to light, the penalties for the teacher will be severe.

My investigation into the conduct of Teacher B. began by interviewing students and consulting with their attorneys who sometimes requested that they be allowed to speak on behalf of their student clients. The most serious allegations I initially encountered were when one student stated that his relationship with Teacher B. began with her paying him compliments about his personal appearance and soon advanced to her giving him rides to and from school and later progressed to sexual involvement. He also stated that after he graduated from high school, Teacher B. took him on a trip to Disney World and allowed him to live with her and her husband for more than a year. These unusual allegations struck me as bizarre, but further investigation proved that the student's allegations were probably accurate.

Teacher B.'s attorney, when asked to respond to this student's allegations, argued that the student fabricated his allegations because Teacher B. and her husband threw him out of their house. Teacher B. asserted that she had allowed the student to live at her home because he was "troubled." She also asserted that over time the boy had become "like a part of their family," until they saw a different side of him and asked him to leave. According to Teacher B., it was at that time that he threatened or vowed to get back at them.

A second student's complaints against Teacher B. regarding sexual involvement were more straightforward. In this case, the student produced examples of clearly inappropriate correspondence from the teacher indicating a more than professional relationship and probable romantic involvement. Accordingly, I recommended to the Westwood School Committee that Teacher B. be terminated from her position, a recommendation the School Committee unanimously accepted. Subsequently, Teacher B. appealed her termination and requested a closed hearing with the Committee.

On the morning this meeting was scheduled, three hours of discussion with her attorney ensued, and the Westwood School Committee attorneys and I agreed to allow Teacher B. to resign "for cause" but required her to forfeit her teaching certificate permanently.   The Westwood School Committee, in allowing her to resign, had rescinded its earlier termination decision. Committee members, however, stated they did not regret having to void their earlier decision since they had achieved their goal of keeping Teacher B. out of the classroom. I thought this to be a reasonable outcome to a clearly unfortunate set of circumstances. Teacher B., on the other hand, continued to maintain her innocence and argued that she agreed to settle the complaints against her rather than defend herself at a potentially humiliating hearing before the school committee.

This case, although extraordinarily devastating for the parties involved, however, did not create the districtwide stress and tension experienced concerning a third sexually related issue in Westwood. This case involved allegations by two female high school students that their male teacher, Teacher C., had inappropriately touched them in class thus creating a hostile classroom environment.

The students, more specifically, indicated that it was this teacher's custom to rub their shoulders and touch their arms and legs in a manner that made them feel uncomfortable. Both students filed complaints with the Westwood police.   Upon learning of these allegations, I immediately placed Teacher C. on administrative leave with pay and initiated my investigation by questioning the students who lodged the complaints while offering the teacher the opportunity to explain what may have occurred.   Teacher C.'s colleagues were outraged. How could I proceed with an investigation, they asked. Teacher C. was a respected veteran professional who may be "a little touchy/feely" now and then, but he was not one to prey on young girls, many told me. Complicating matters, Teacher C. was very popular with students, in general, and attended and participated in many extracurricular activities. Teacher C., in short, had many supporters while I and the students filing complaints had few. Faculty support for Teacher C., in fact, was so strong that many began wearing yellow ribbons to school as symbolic support for their banished colleague.

As tensions between superintendent and staff grew, I made an error that made matters even worse. My investigation continued and the school year was proceeding to a close when the high school faculty requested that I meet with them as a group to discuss Teacher C. On the same day, I also received a call from a statewide newspaper reporter who asked me what I was doing to address faculty unrest regarding my handling of the Teacher C. matter. I replied to the reporter that I had received a request from the faculty to attend a meeting with them that was scheduled for the following afternoon in the high school auditorium at 2:00 P.M.

Approximately sixty teachers were in attendance at the meeting that afternoon when the high school principal noticed the reporter whom I had spoken to earlier at the back of the room. The principal felt obligated to inform the faculty of the reporter's presence. All but two faculty members immediately rose from their seats and walked out of the auditorium.

At the time, I had not even thought of my comments to the reporter about the scheduling of this meeting, and I was clearly surprised and taken aback by the faculty walkout. My approach throughout this and any similar investigations was to be as open as possible with media and the public while working to maintain the confidentiality rights of the involved parties. My intent was to convey that the Westwood School Department considered all sexual misconduct complaints to be serious and to avoid the perception that my investigations were "whitewashes." I actually thought that clearing the air in the reporter's presence might be a good idea. The faculty thought just the opposite. During my conversation with the union leadership after the walkout, I learned that the teachers had different ideas as to the meeting's agenda. They especially wanted to know why I could not have simply handled the matter of Teacher C. more routinely without interviewing students and staff in a manner that the faculty considered overly aggressive and accusatory.

The afternoon following the walkout, I met with the high school's faculty, without a reporter in attendance, and learned more about their concerns. Flash points during the meeting reflected faculty concerns that I should have been more of an advocate for Teacher C. during the investigatory process and less focused on the rights of the students who may have filed their complaints as a way of retaliating against the teacher for having given them poor grades.

I addressed these faculty concerns by agreeing that their perceptions were relevant, but that the issue of unprofessional conduct was of uppermost importance. I also stated that if I had to err on one side on a close judgment call, it was my responsibility to protect students' rights and guarantee them a safe and professional school environment. Accordingly, it was my duty to be a student advocate. Subsequently I learned from the union leadership that my last statement was one of the worst I could have made and that it added fuel to the teachers' anger about my handling of the investigation. I was now angry as well. Being a superintendent, however, has taught me the importance of clear vision and a cool head.

DeBruyn notes, "Things can go wrong even in the best organization. The best managers are often known for the way they handle people problems." I have also learned that most likely when an issue first surfaces, only the tip of the iceberg appears. One must explore what is not immediately apparent and talk to others who may be in a position to relay important facts. It is also safe to assume that each person involved will tend to present the case from his or her point of view, which may or may not reflect reality. I later realized as I thought about my comments at the faculty meeting, that I might have been a bit more temperate in my remarks about being a child advocate and that although my remarks were correct, I was probably expressing them at the wrong time.

These actions, however, did not end my involvement with the case. The families of the student victims retained legal counsel and requested that the minimum their children receive be free tuition to another high school of their choice.

These requests were referred to the district's insurance carrier, and a long trail of negotiations with the parties and their attorneys began. Complicating matters was the fact that the two victims knew one another and that they and their attorneys shared information regarding their respective situations which while similar differed in certain respects.

As negotiations progressed among the parties, the Westwood School Department and I acknowledged the inappropriateness of Teacher C.'s behavior, but our legal counsel advised us that the school department's greatest liability involved the high school faculty's reactions to my disciplinary action against Teacher C. and their wearing yellow ribbons in protest. The faculty, by wearing the ribbons, left themselves and the school department open to a claim that a hostile environment had been created for the student complainants. One teacher, in addition, had admonished one of the young women for even raising a complaint.

From the victims' perspective, negotiations were further complicated by the fact that the district's insurance carrier was willing to pay for the students' out-of-district tuitions, but only if their parents released the Westwood School Department and its agents from liability. Furthermore, the parents were asked by the insurance carrier to assume the costs of transporting their children to school.

As these discussions progressed, I learned a great deal about how insurance companies and attorneys negotiate and the give and take associated with their adversarial positions. Amicable discussions occurred for the most part as I assumed the role of ambassador to the parents, constantly attempting to keep lines of communication open.

At the time of this writing, a final release agreement has been reached with one set of parents whereby the insurance company agreed to pay out-of-district tuition costs, transportation costs, the parents' legal fees, and compensation for the parents' lost wages. Release agreements for the other two students are still in the process of negotiation, and the insurance carrier has assumed their out-of-district tuition costs.

An important lesson I would like to convey resulting from my experience with these types of cases is the importance of comprehensive, ongoing staff training. While definition of sexual harassment issues and policy clarifications are paramount, an additional training topic that must be stressed involves faculty reaction to complaints. A neutral attitude is required, and all staff must be aware that any behavior on their part that hints of retaliation against complainants will not be tolerated. It is a teacher's obligation to make school environments safe, reasonable, and comfortable, even if a student has lodged what some faculty members may consider an unfair complaint against a colleague. The merit of student complaints are to be decided by a higher authority.

Chapter 10

Cycles of Leadership Change

I am reassured as I compose this last chapter that grounding my work in an adaptive or protean theme was a good choice. The changes that occurred during my first three years in Westwood were greater than I could have anticipated.

During the period 1996-1999, my administrative team of fifteen turned over so frequently that as of June 30, 1999, only five of the original fifteen remained. One moved to another district, one was promoted to another position, one was terminated, and seven retired. What can I say about continuity in administrative structure?

Additionally, there are now twenty-four new teachers and ninety others in new positions resulting primarily from retirements. The ebb and flow of teachers from one position to another is difficult to comprehend for those not intimately involved with the educational process. Keeping track of personnel assignments is a major administrative task requiring thousands of hours. The results of such changes can be both positive and negative.

Teachers who are in need of new challenges have the opportunity to experiment, learn and develop new instructional methods, work with different colleagues, and make new acquaintances. Change enables teachers to grow and evolve professionally. Changes from an administrator's perspective, however, can impede his ability to evaluate the effectiveness of new teaching strategies and curriculum.

Westwood was fortunate to attract experienced administrators to help make the adjustment to these changes. In politics and professional and college sports, an accepted maxim is that a leader needs to have his/her "own people" in place, when new agendas and policies are implemented. Consequently, I was fortunate to recruit experienced and well-regarded former colleagues who received School Committee approval to fill administrative posts in Westwood. The positions they assumed included Assistant Principal of Westwood High School, Principal of Maisie Quinn Elementary School, and School Improvement Leader. These experienced administrators made and continue to make strong contributions to the continuity and team oriented approach I have tried to establish, but the complexities of the ongoing Rhode Island reform movement presented us with many challenges.

Diane Ravitch, one of my favorite educational commentators, in "Life-and-Death Musings--What If

Research Really Mattered?" (*Education Week*, December 12, 1998) offers a humorous critique of the current state of educational research and reform when she compares its development and application to more reliable and more sophisticated medical research in the United States.

Ravitch, while being treated for a pulmonary embolism in a New York City hospital, reflects on how the physicians were so confident in their treatment of her ailment--their certainty based on many previous successes in similar situations. She also wonders, however, what the attitude of educational experts would be in a similar situation.

She humorously notes, "As compared to the medical experts, the 'educational' experts would begin to argue over whether anything was actually wrong with me." She states, "A few might think that I had a problem, but others would scoff and say that such an analysis was tantamount to 'blaming the victim.' Some would challenge the concept of 'illness,' claiming that it was a social construction, utterly lacking in objective reality. Others would reject the evidence of the tests used to diagnose my ailment, a few would say the tests were meaningless for females, and others would insist that the tests were meaningless for anyone under any circumstances. One of the noisier researchers, in fact, would maintain that any effort to focus attention on my individual situation would merely divert attention from gross social injustices." Among the raucous crowd of educational experts, Ravitch suggests ". . . there would be no agreement, no common set of standards for diagnosing problems."

I agree with Ravitch and go on to add that one of the biggest obstacles to school improvement faced by superintendents is the lack of clear and authoritatively researched priorities for change in public schools acceptable to school committee members, teachers, and parents. Previous chapters have sketched the cyclical nature of the school improvement process, which needs to be viewed as part of a continuum of trial, effort, learning, change, and redirection with a clear focus on faculty professional development.

I have emphasized throughout this discussion that schools must become more sensitive, accepting, and supportive of individual student learning styles. To this end, it was also stressed that there must be a shared vision among superintendents, staff, administrators, parents, and school board members as to the pace and direction of progress.

Educational reform, for many, oftentimes is a continuum of the "same old, same old" accompanied by an agenda of narrow political interests. Completing my third year as superintendent in Westwood, I am sometimes reminded of my experience as assistant superintendent in Wellton where the agenda was dominated by budget problems, conflict, and divisiveness and fear that history may repeat itself. Presently, only two of the original five member board that hired me remain on the Westwood School Committee. One member was defeated in the 1996 election, one in 1998, and another decided not to seek reelection. During this period, I also experienced the leadership of three different school committee chairs. Each of the first two chairpersons had his own priorities, agenda, and leadership style and I am presently learning the style and priorities of the new chair. This situation is all too common in local school districts across the country as politics and lack of continuity in leadership slow and impede educational reform.

The National School Board Association clearly emphasizes that the role of school committee leadership is to ensure that meetings are run by rules of order and that the board has established agendas, goals, and objectives. The chairs I have worked with handled these responsibilities well, although differently. The challenges I faced while working with different chairs related to their priorities for the district and their methods of understanding and articulating the expectations of their fellow board members.

An effective board meeting for a superintendent, according to the National School Board Association, is one that provides no surprises, unexpected questions, attacks, or crises. Some board members, on the other hand, might prefer a bit more of a politically charged contentious environment. After all, they are politicians!

The first chair I worked with in Westwood was strongly focused on technology, worked in a technology related field, and would often pose well-meaning, but unanticipated, technology-related questions at board meetings. As a father of young children, he also had a strong interest in early childhood education. Most often, he worked behind the scenes with fellow board members to obtain consensus on agenda items resulting in orderly and professional meetings.

The 1996 election served as the impetus for the installation of a new chair with a complementary agenda, but one with an important adjunct. The new chair had been a long-term political activist, candidate for statewide political office, and was a charismatic, eloquent, and at times caustic and bombastic leader. He epitomized hands-on control while his predecessor had been somewhat detached in his leadership style. As a longtime resident and political activist in Westwood and director of the town's community service center, he seemed to know of every crime, economic circumstance, political controversy, and rumor in the community. His energy, interest, and commitment as a school committee member were all-encompassing.

At first I found him to be overbearing and often thought that he was attempting to usurp my role. In time, I learned to appreciate his talents and eventually recognized him to be a major force whenever progressive innovations were made in the district. One of his great strengths was his ability and willingness to be in almost constant communication with his fellow board members, town council leadership, and me. He always, in effect, seemed to find a way to accomplish what he believed to be in the best interest of the school district. While he was re-elected to the Westwood School Committee in 1998, he lost his chairmanship through lack of political support.

The superintendent/school board relationship is fragile, and I am working at fostering new positive relationships. The present situation is sometimes difficult. Often a superintendent when working with a new school board is, if only by inference, associated with the policies and politics of prior boards. Superintendents, as a rule, attempt to build positive relationships with new boards, and it is important that they meet with new members and provide them with the background information they need to function effectively in their new roles.

In April, 1999, the Westwood School Committee provided me with a positive performance evaluation and extended my contract for a three-year period, the maximum length provided by Rhode Island law, resulting in my becoming one of the highest paid superintendents in the state. The Westwood School

Committee and I, however, still remain cautious about the future of the district's school improvement plans.

A recent report of the Rhode Island Public Expenditure Council (1999), highlights how the state has embarked upon an ambitious educational reform agenda. It has been well-documented that demographic trends in Rhode Island and related research suggest that unless the state commits itself to investing in early intervention and support systems for children born to poverty, disadvantaged children in communities such as Westwood and Wellton will continue to fail and drop out of high school in even greater numbers.

In simple terms, the gap between the "haves" and the "have nots" continues to grow in small cities and towns across the country. Pressures on superintendents to meet the ever-increasing social and educational needs of students, as the public's willingness or ability to pay diminishes, can be overwhelming and often determine the length of a superintendent's tenure. Negotiations are sometimes volatile, and oftentimes the public's misconceptions about schools rise to the surface. Teacher "bashing" can result as people rail about their high salaries and the absence of progress in improving student achievement.

The Westwood Town Charter stipulates that a school budget must be submitted to the town council on February 1st of each new fiscal year beginning July 1st. During my first two years in the town, financial circumstances were relatively good, and public scrutiny of school finances was not overburdening. At this writing, however, I am not so optimistic. My initial 1999 budget included a revenue shortfall of some $1.6 million and the town government initially projected no help in addressing it. An unanticipated 10% plus increase in health care costs was a major cause of the problem.

As I lobbied for increased state aid to meet this looming deficit, my concern grew that school committee members and town residents would become increasingly acrimonious and skeptical about the investments in educational reform that we had been making. Funding for improvements such as a Professional Development Academy and alternative school programs were being resisted, and I wondered if I would re-experience the negativity I had encountered during my days in Wellton. The problem resulted from the formula used by the state to fund local education budgets.

In Chapter 5, I briefly discussed school finance issues and Wenglinsky's work on related policy concerns focusing on disparities between low-income and more affluent school districts. The problem is for the most part a state and national one, as he suggests, with different states assuming varying levels of responsibility for local education costs.

Rhode Island at present does comparatively well in the amount it spends on public education. In a recent evaluation of state education policy by *Education Week* (Wolk, 1999), the state ranks fifteenth in the nation, with its per pupil expenditure of $6,468.00, adjusted for inflation and regional cost differences. Like many other states, however, Rhode Island's method of financing was rated in this study as inequitable and unfair, and ranked only twenty-third nationally thus shifting school funding burdens to local government bodies.

The Westwood school system is labor intensive, a condition shared by all school districts. Eighty-three percent of its 1999-2000 budget is proposed to fund salaries and benefits, and a twelve-percent increase in health insurance costs is projected. Included in the 1999-2000 budget were the costs of three new programs: (1) a self-contained, high school program for learning disabled students; (2) a pre-school program for students diagnosed as behaviorally disordered; and 3) a self-contained alternative program for middle school students. Realignment of Westwood's K-12 curriculum was also established as a major priority.

The school committee and I lobbied long and hard with the Westwood Town Council and state legislators to fund these new initiatives. Focusing on the relationship between investment in public education and real estate values, we were able to convince the town to devote an additional $500,000.00 to the 1999-2000 budget, and the state responded to our $1.6 million projected deficit by appropriating an additional $969,000.00. These appropriations, however, simply covered increased salary and benefit costs and did not take into consideration program improvements, textbooks, and other instructional materials.

The Professional Development Academy survived this budget battle since it had been included as a negotiated item in the existing teachers' union contract, but the time allotted for annual mandatory training for teachers had to be trimmed from thirty to fifteen hours. Other initiatives such as the expansion of the alternative school program and curriculum realignment plans, however, remained unfunded. Some progress had been made, but the Westwood School Committee, the administrative team, and I were frustrated. As is common in many low-income communities, educational progress in Westwood seemed to be too closely tied to local budgetary problems, property values, and tax rates.

Budgetary concerns common to public school districts in the United States continued to plague my tenure in Westwood as efforts were made to implement a comprehensive systemwide reform agenda. These concerns included structural impediments to recruiting quality teachers and administrators.

The cases of three potential teaching candidates dramatically illustrate the teacher recruitment problem. The first two henceforth referred to as those of Michelle and Michael illustrate how teacher union contracts, state teacher certification requirements, and the inflexibility of both come together to hinder educational reform.

Michelle is a 1990's graduate of the University of Rhode Island. She majored in both mathematics and computer science and graduated with honors. She is an attractive, personable young woman with a natural ability to work with young people and would make an excellent, if not extraordinary, high school mathematics teacher. On a number of occasions, I observed Michelle teaching computer classes to adults; she exuded the enthusiasm and sensitivity to her students' individual needs and personalities, a talent crucial to a good high school teacher.

The budgetary realities governing teacher recruitment make attracting Michelle to the profession almost impossible. Michelle, a thirty something, currently works as a computer programmer at a hospital affiliated with Brown University. Her annual salary is in the $65,000.00 range and because her computer programming talents are in demand, she can make her own weekly schedule. No school bells, recess duty, or lunch supervision for Michelle. She reports to a university professor whose only basic directive is "Accomplish what we need and on deadline, and your schedule is your own." This flexibility allows Michelle to own and operate her own computer programming consulting business and earn additional tens of thousands of dollars.

Michelle would be a welcome addition to any high school mathematics department, however offering her a starting first-step salary of $30,000.00 cannot match the current realities of her employment market. Possibly, if she were offered a salary of $52,000.00 paid to teachers with ten years of experience, she might consider it a competitive offer; school committee/teacher contract agreements, however, prohibit such an offer. Michelle will likely continue her career in the private sector, and students will miss the opportunity of benefiting from her multifaceted background.

The case of Michael, while different in many ways, illustrates similar economic realities which impede educational reform. Michael, also a 1990's college graduate, completed the teacher education program in English at Boston College and graduated with honors. Michael always wanted to be a teacher and taught English for a year in Africa. His African experiences broadened his outlook and matured him, thus making him a likely candidate for successful high school teaching in the United States. In addition to his background, Michael, like Michelle, is charismatic and personable.

Unlike Michelle, Michael initially desired a career in public education and taught English last year in one of Rhode Island's poorest and most difficult high schools. He taught students identified as at risk of failure, improved their scores on statewide tests, was well-respected by his colleagues and principal, and received positive performance evaluations.

After his successful first year of teaching, Michael asked his principal for a substantial raise, at least $4,500.00, or fifteen percent of his salary. Michael was politely informed by his principal that this would be impossible. He was told that according to contract, he would receive the same salary increase as every other first year teacher--four percent or about $1,200.00. No performance-based bonuses were possible. Every first-year teacher would receive the same increase.

Michael was disturbed by this fact and thought that somehow his performance should be rewarded. He knew of teachers who had not been successful in their first year, had poor classroom management skills, and "just were not good teachers," but would receive the same four percent increase. It bothered him that everyone was treated alike. He was also frustrated when he compared himself to his sister who had just completed her graduate education, was employed as an optometrist, and was earning close to a "six-figure" income. Michael knew he was working just as hard but had no hope within the current teacher compensation system to match his sister's lifestyle. He wanted to marry, buy a house, and raise a family and could not see his way clear to do so on his teacher's salary. Regrettably, Michael's talents were lost to the teaching profession; he became a financial analyst in New York and doubled his income in his first year. His economic future is bright. He would have been a great teacher!

The third teaching candidate is Ralph. Ralph is at a different stage in his career compared to Michelle and Michael. He earned his Ph.D. in chemistry from Brown University in the early 1980's; served as a teaching assistant at Brown, receiving positive evaluations; and taught mathematics at a private high school.

Upon completing his doctoral training, Ralph forged a successful career in private industrial research, earning salaries well into the six figures, traveled a great deal, and published his research in numerous professional journals. Having accomplished most of his career goals, he now wants to return to high school teaching in Rhode Island. The problem is that Rhode Island, like many states, will not acknowledge his work experience or education, in terms of his certifiability to teach. To teach high school in Rhode Island, Ralph would have to take a number of teacher education courses, student teach, and probably return to teaching at the first salary step. The impediments are understandably too much for him to overcome. Ralph is not likely to return to high school teaching. His return to the classroom would be valuable. His research, industrial and practical experience, and Ph.D. would greatly benefit high school students. The current system, however, makes his return unlikely.

Problems related to the recruitment of teachers also affect the hiring of quality principals and administrators especially in urban areas. Amy Klein and Drake Witham (1999) write of the difficulties currently experienced in Rhode Island's largest metropolitan school district. Part of the Rhode Island dilemma in recruiting quality administrators, as they suggest, is that it borders the state of Connecticut where school administrator salaries average $10,000.00-$15,000.00 per year higher. Administrative recruitment efforts in Westwood have also been hampered by the fact that teacher salaries are among the highest in Rhode Island and are supplemented by educational background and longevity increments. Department chairpersons, for example, with ten years experience and a master's degree work 190 days per year and earn about $3,000 less than assistant principals who work an additional twenty days. The difference in salary is not enough to convince enough teachers to rise to the administrative ranks because of increased compensation.

Hardy (1998) notes that school districts across the nation are trying a variety of strategies to find and attract teachers and administrators -- and keep them once they're hired. Some Texas school districts offer signing bonuses to hard-to-find instructors in mathematics and bilingual education; more than forty states offer alternative certification for people in other careers who want to pursue teaching. In Connecticut, school districts provide incentive compensation, perhaps modeled after Fortune 500 companies, to retain quality superintendents. One of these approaches, for example, makes substantial annual deposits to a trust established on behalf of the superintendent. If the superintendent remains in the district for a designated number of years, five for example, the full value of the trust is assigned to him. If he leaves prior to five years, the school district retains the trust. Such creative compensation approaches, however, have yet to be implemented in Rhode Island.

A recent study by the Cooperative Institutional Research Program at the University of California at Los Angeles (U.C.L.A.) (*New York Times*, July 11, 1999) provides some hope that national trends in teacher education programs may have positive effects. The survey, first conducted in 1966, polls 300,000 freshmen at over 600 American colleges and universities each year about their lives and interests, including what they want to do after graduation. While the survey does not reflect actual career choices, the 1998 version has shown signs of renewed student interest in teaching. According to this study, the number of bachelor's and master's degrees in education rose thirty-one percent from 1986 to 1996, the last year available, compared with twenty-two percent in other fields. This trend is also apparent at some of the nation's elite institutions. At Princeton University, for example, the number of students enrolled in its teacher preparation programs has risen to twenty-five from five since 1990. The number of applications to the teacher education programs at Columbia University has risen to more than 830 in 1999, up from 700 in 1994.

Many career counselors say part of the reason for the current increased interest in the teaching profession is that there seems to be a mood among students on college campuses to assume significant challenges and make differences in the lives of others. According to other experts, however, despite indications of growing interest in teaching and administration, the realities of these jobs can still be discouraging, especially in urban areas.

Reflecting upon my early experiences as an assistant and superintendent of schools, I realize that I probably would have opted for another career had I followed the traditional path of teacher, principal, and superintendent over a twenty to thirty year career. The fact that I was an outsider assuming the role of a school district leader, I believe, has served me well.

The demanding pace and lack of public support and recognition for educators all too often stultify the spirit and diminish creativity. Better paths of career mobility must be found for those interested in public school work. Offering credit for other types of employment in terms of both seniority with regard to teacher contracts and retirement plans would be helpful. These issues are especially salient for minorities interested in serving in public schools and talented individuals from all walks of life.

School critics often suggest that teachers must change; I offer the challenge that the public must change the way it views schools. For the most part, teachers and administrators are working as hard as they can with the knowledge base they possess. An infusion of new ideas and perspectives is definitely needed; however, critics also need to understand what is happening in schools and who the people are who dedicate their lives to them.

At the conclusion of his book, *Redesigning School-- Lessons for the 21st Century*, McDonald (1996) recalls the following anecdote:

"I found myself standing in a luncheon line just in front of an old teacher of mine. We were inching our way toward the cold cuts, and he asked what I was working on. I told him about the book, *Redesigning School*. 'What do you call it?' he asked at once. '*Redesigning School*,' I answered.

"'Wrong image,' he chided. 'What do you mean?' I asked. 'Sounds like blueprints, and you're the one drawing them,' he stated. 'No,' I protested. 'The book redefines design.' " McDonald concludes that he and his teacher reached the cold cuts, and their conversation trailed off. The question, however, as to who would be most successful in redesigning schools remained open. McDonald's answer might be, "Yes, we can have improved schools in the twenty-first century that teach all children to use their minds well, but only if we really want such schools and then only if we reorient our common sense about how to get there."

School redesign or reform, he adds, should be the uppermost priority of the people closest to the children, and support of their activities must be provided by local, state, and national leadership.

I agree with McDonald and further emphasize the need for a common sense approach to school reform. During my five short years as a superintendent, I have found that fostering a common sense vision, mission, and goals among school committee, superintendent, teachers, parents, and other constituencies is the greatest challenge for an educational leader.

In "Us? Set Goals?" Bell and Harris (1999) recount the transformation of superintendent/school board relationships in the Bensalem (PA) Township that is relevant to most people involved in education. The authors describe that district's situation as follows: "Four years ago, you could sit outside the room where the school board was holding an executive session and get a pretty good idea of what was going on--they were shouting that loudly."

Board members promoted their own political agendas, and the administration felt obliged to accommodate their pet causes or demands. Nit picking, mistrust, and suspicion ran rampant at most board meetings, and micromanagement approached the absurd. The situation deteriorated to the point that when a paving contractor was having trouble meeting the district's specifications for resurfacing a parking lot, one board member took it upon herself to measure the depth of the asphalt. Contentious dissension also surfaced regarding the hiring practices for teachers and administrators. Finger pointing and suspicion between board members and administrators were rampant, and the general tenor of the district was negative. What turned Bensalem around?

The community formulated a steering committee for change consisting of the superintendent, assistant superintendent, and the school board vice president. In many ways, these three individuals were at the center of the district's conflicts and subsequently became the focus of their resolution.

I began this book by emphasizing that superintendents and leaders of any complex organization must often abandon expectations of control and recognize there are different ways to solve problems. Conciliation, appreciation, and support for the work of others are usually the keys to success.

For members of the Bensalem steering committee, building a psychologically safe and trusting environment was the key to moving the district forward. In effect, the structure of interaction in the town leadership circle had been so damaged in recent years it had to be rebuilt by improving the basic human skills of listening, communication, and collaboration. A summary of the Bensalem's steering committee's solution follows:

- Work hard at reaching consensus.
- Be willing to listen to others.
- Point no fingers.
- Look only to the future and do not dwell on the past.

I can only wonder how these messages would serve me if I were to someday return as Wellton's superintendent.

Certainly, there are no easy answers as one contemplates the future of schools and their administration. To conclude, let me return to my earlier reference to Samuelson's *The Good Life and Its Discontents.* Samuelson, as mentioned, addresses the question why the United States, the most powerful and most democratic nation in the world is so often overcome by self-doubt and confusion.   Questioning today's fashionable pessimism regarding public institutions, he argues that the United States has experienced great success since the Second World War, creating unprecedented prosperity and permitting more Americans than ever before to seek the American dream. He also asks, however, "Then why is it that so many of us feel so bad about our institutions?" He suggests that the answer lies in a paradox of our own making. Perhaps we are to some extent disillusioned -- "not because we have done so little but because we often expect too much too soon."

In Chapter 1, I referred to Schorr's analysis of the success of compensatory education programs like Head Start that have begun to close some of the gaps between the educational "haves" and "have-nots."   Too often, however, these successes do not receive the public attention they deserve. Part of the problem, as I mention in Chapter 7, is that the media often focuses public attention solely on the negatives associated with schools.

James Comer recently stated, "The media reporting, in my opinion, is a significant part of the education problem. The tone is almost always about the bad. And you can call the press about the good things, and they don't want to hear it. They're not interested; it's not a story."

While I partially agree with Comer, I also suggest that those responsible for administering schools take a proactive and unified approach in promoting their positions.   Educational reform is taking place. Sometimes too slowly for many, but progress is occurring. Trust and cooperation among the partners--

parents, teachers, administrators, school board members, students, and the general public--are the keys to success.

Recently a number of reform advocates argued that strong consideration should be given to abolishing current school board/school committee governance structures. That is, strong consideration should be given to abolishing local school committees and implementing cross-country or multi-committee collaborative public education governance structures in all states.

At present, New York's strong regent system is considered more effective than the decentralized approach favored in Rhode Island where I have served as a superintendent. My experience, however, has been that strong local school boards can, and often do, serve positive functions. The National School Board Association (1996) observes that despite their basic commonalties, school boards differ in the complexities of the communities they serve and the personalities on the board.

Board membership, nationally, averages five or seven members but varies from as few as three to as many as fifteen. Almost all school boards are elected, but a few (less than 3 percent) are appointed. Enrollments, budgets, staff, and school facilities run the gamut in size and complexity from the one- or two-school system to the huge metropolitan systems of New York, Chicago, and Los Angeles.

The National School Board Association rhetorically asked, "What forces produced the social entities we call school boards?" The answers, the Association says, lie in our history and in our continued thrust for representative government. The roots of local school control by lay people reach back to the town meetings of New England settlements and to the resolve of the pioneers and householders to establish schools. Given this tradition, it is no wonder that school board and superintendent relationships often continue to be contentious.

The National School Board Association (1996) maintains that from their very inception, school committees had no easy time. Some colonists neither welcomed schools nor rushed to their support despite laws enacted by the colonies encouraging or compelling school attendance. Yet, the first school committees carried on with determination. First, they had to locate a place to hold classes. Then, they had to find an adult who could read and write and who was willing to become schoolmaster. Providing food and lodging for the schoolmaster and keeping the schoolhouse in repair and heated were also tasks assigned to school committees. In most cases, they probably performed the actual physical work to accomplish these goals. In some ways, their efforts make our current roles seem a lot easier.

The National School Board Association (1996) goes on to observe, "Hemmed in by increasing legislative and legal mandates on the one hand and by critics and pressure groups on the other, local school boards may seem a helpless anachronism." The Association concludes, however, that nothing is further from the truth. "If school boards did not exist, a wise observer once said, the American public would have to invent them -- just as it did two hundred years ago." In essence, today's school boards, challenged though they are, fulfill the American public's enduring desire to keep schools close to the people. To this, I add, "Superintendents who forget this fact are almost certainly doomed to failure!"

REFERENCES

Alvarado, A. "Professional Development Is The Job." *American Educator*, Winter, 1998.

Andrews v. Philadelphia, 895 F.2d 1469 (3rd Cir. 1990)

Becker, H. *Sociological Work: Method and Substance.* Aldine Publishing Co., 1970.

Bell, D. *The Coming of Post Industrial Society--A Venture in Social Forecasting.* Basic Books, Inc., 1976.

Bell, R., and Harris, J. "Governance: Us? Set Goals?" *American School Board Journal*, July 1999.

Benziger, K. *The BTSA User Manual.* The Human Resource Technology Co., 1994.

Bouton v. BMW of North America, Inc., 1994 U.S. App. Lexis 20755 (3rd Cir., 65 Emp. Proc. Guide (CCH) 43,185

Bowles, S. and Gintis, H. *Schooling in Capitalist America: educational reform and the contradictions of economic life.* Basic Books, Inc. 1976.

Center for The Study of Sports in Society. Northeastern University, 1998.

Comer, J. P. *Waiting For A Miracle--Why Schools Can't Solve Our Problems And How We Can.* Dutton, 1997.

Cooper, M.J. "Probing for Truth: Investigating Charges of Sexual Misconduct." *American School Board Journal,* September, 1998.

Crisci, G.S. "When No Means No." *American School Board Journal,* June, 1999.

Daley, B. "Homework Losing Its Way Home." *The Boston Globe,* November 10, 1998.

DeBruyn, R.L. "Getting Board Approval." *Superintendents Only,* Volume 6 No. 2, October, 1998.

DeBruyn, R.L. *Superintendents Only,* Vol. 5 No. 3, November 1997.

Deming, W.E. (1993), The New Economics for Industry, Government, and Education. MIT Center for Advanced Engineering Study.

Drury, D.W. *Reinventing School-Based Management -- A School Board Guide to School-Based Improvement*, National School Boards Association, 1999.

Evans, R. *The Human Side of School Change--Reform, Resistance, and the Real-Life Problems of Innovations.* Jossey-Bass, 1996.

Fullan, M., and Miles, M. "Getting Reform Right: What Works and What Doesn't." *Phi Delta Kappan*, June 1992.

Gill, B., and Schlossman, S. "A Sin Against Childhood: Progressive Education and the Crusade to Abolish Homework, 1897-1941." *American Journal of Education*, Nov. 1996.

Hardy, L. "A Good Teacher is Hard To Find -- The Kids are Beating Down The Doors -- Will You Find Enough Qualified People to Teach Them?" *The American School Board Journal*, Sept. 1998.

Hofferth, S. "Children's Time." University of Michigan Institute for Social Research, 1998.

Huberman, M. "Recipes for Busy Kitchens." Knowledge: Creation, Diffusion, Utilization, 1983, 4.

Indicators for Monitoring Mathematics and Science Education, A Sourcebook. Rand Corporation, 1989.

Information Works! S.A.L.T. Survey Report. National

Center on Public Education and Social Policy, 1998.

Jackson, P. *Life in Classrooms*. Holt, Rinehart & Winston, 1968.

Jencks, C. and Phillips, M. *The Black-White Test Score Gap*. The Brookings Institution, 1998.

Jentz, B. *Entry: The Hiring, Start-Up, and Supervision of Administrators*. Donnelley and Sons, 1982.

Klein, A., and Witham, D. "Strong demand, short supply for school superintendents." *Providence Journal*, Feb. 21, 1999

Kralovec, E. and Buell, J. "Rethinking Homework." *The Boston Globe*, Nov. 13, 1998.

Leithwood, K. and Menzies, T. "Forms and Effects of School-Based Management: A Review." *Educational Policy*, 12 (3), 1998.

Levy, F. *The New Dollars and Dreams: American Incomes and Economic Change*. The Russell Sage Foundation, 1998.

Lieberman, E., "Ex-legislator charged with assault in confrontation with grid coach." *Providence Journal*, May 24, 1999.

Lieberman, E., "West Warwick besieged by misconduct

reports." *Providence Journal*, June 13, 1998.

Lifton, R.J. *The Protean Self: Human Resilience in an Age of Fragmentation*. Basic Books, 1993.

McDonald, J. *Redesigning School: Lessons for the 21st Century*. Jossey Bass, 1996.

McGee, M. "School Based Evaluation: A Comprehensive Self-Help Guide." National School Board Association, 1998.

Merton, R. *The Idea of Social Structure*. Harcourt Brace Jovanovich, 1975.

Milman vs. The Barrington School Committee. Rhode Island Commissioner of Education's Decision, 1980.

Munsch, R. and Martchenko, M. *Show and Tell*. Annick Press Ltd., 1991.

National School Boards Association. *Becoming A Better School Board Member*. National School Board Association, 1996.

National School Boards Association. *Raising The Bar: A School Board Primer on Student Achievement*. National School Board Association, 1990.

National School Boards Association. *Reaching for*

Excellence: What Local School Districts Are Doing To Raise Student Achievement, 1998.

Northeast And Islands Regional Educational Laboratory at Brown University. *Study of Dropouts At West Warwick High School.* July, 1997.

Oncken, W. and Wass, D. "Management Time: Who's Got The Monkey?" *Harvard Business Review.* Nov.-Dec. 1974.

Organization for Economic Cooperation and Development (OECD), Directorate for Education, Employment, Labor and Social Affairs, Education Committee, "Effectiveness of Schooling and Educational Resource Management: Synthesis of County Studies," Parts 22 and 23, 1994.

Phi Delta Kappa/Gallup Poll of the Public's Attitudes toward Public Schools, 1998.

Ravitch, D. "Life-and-Death Musings -- What if Research Really Mattered?" *Education Week*, Dec. 16, 1998

Raywid, M.A. "Finding Time For Collaboration." *Educational Leadership* Vol. 51, No. 1, September, 1993.

Reeves, D.B. "Holding Principals Accountable." *The School Administrator*, October, 1998.

Reynolds, B. *Glory Days: On Sports, Men and Dreams That*

Don't Die. St. Martin's Press, 1998.

Rhode Island Department of Education. *Measuring Rhode Island Schools for Changes.*

Rhode Island Education Laws and Rules Annotated. Micnie, 1996-1997.

Rhode Island Public Expenditure Council. *Results: Education in Rhode Island.* Rhode Island Public Expenditure Council, 1999.

Samuelson, R.J. *The Good Life And Its Discontents: The American Dream In The Age of Entitlement.* Times Books. Random House, 1995.

Sarason, S.B. *The Creation of Settings and The Future of Societies.* Jossey Bass, 1972.

Schorr, L.B. *Common Purpose: Strengthening Families and Neighborhoods To Rebuild America.* Anchor Books. Doubleday, 1997.

Senge, P. *The Fifth Discipline: The Art and Practice of The Learning Organization.* Doubleday, 1990.

Serrano v. Priest (I) (5 Cal 3d 584, 96 Cal. Rptr. 601, 487 P.2nd 12141 [Calif. 1971])

Shavelson, R.J., McDonald, L. M. and Oakes, J. "Indicators for Monitoring Mathematics and

Science Education." Rand Corporation, 1989.

Sheehy, G. *Passages: Predictable Crises of Adult Life*. E.P. Dutton, 1974.

Sizer, T. *Horace's Compromise: The Dilemma of the American High School*. Houghton Mifflin Co., 1984.

Sizer, T. *Horace's Hope: What Works For The American High School*. Houghton Mifflin Co., 1996.

Stevenson and Stigler. "Common Measures, Indicators of School Success -- Half-Full/Half-Empty." *The American School Board Journal*, December, 1998.

Stringfield, S. "Choosing Success." *American Educator*, Fall, 1998.

Summers, A.A. and Johnson, A.W. "The effects of school-based management plans." E.A. Hanushek and D.W. Jorgenson (Eds.), *Improving America's Schools: The Roles of Incentives*. National Academy Press (1996)

Tabor, M., "Despite Low Prestige and Pay, More Answer The Call To Teach." *New York Times*, July 11, 1999

Ventetuolo v. Burke, 596 F. 2d 476, 480

Wenglinsky, H. *When Money Matters: How Educational Expenditures Improve Student Performance and How*

They Don't. Educational Testing Service, 1997.

Whitty, G. and Power, S. "Quasi-Markets and Curriculum Control: Making Sense of Recent Educational Reforms in England and Wales." *Education Administrator Quarterly,* 33 (2), 1997

Winerip, M., "School Choice A New Beginning for Public Education or the Beginning of the End?" *New York Times Magazine,* Section 6, June 17, 1998.

Winerip, M., "Schools for Sale." *New York Times Magazine,* June 14, 1998.

Winerip, M., "Too Much Too Soon -- Or Is That Too Little Too Late? A Report from the homework front." *The New York Times, Education Life,* January 3, 1999.

Wolk, R. *Education Week: Quality Counts,* 1999.

INDEX